THE CROOKED PATH
TO ABOLITION

THE
CROOKED PATH
TO ABOLITION

Abraham Lincoln and the Antislavery Constitution

JAMES OAKES

W. W. NORTON & COMPANY

Independent Publishers Since 1923

For information about permission to reproduce selections from this book, write to
Permissions, W. W. Norton & Company, Inc., 500 Fifth Avenue, New York, NY 10110

For information about special discounts for bulk purchases, please contact
W. W. Norton Special Sales at specialsales@wwnorton.com or 800-233-4830

Manufacturing by LSC Communications, Harrisonburg
Production manager: Lauren Abbate

Library of Congress Cataloging-in-Publication Data

Names: Oakes, James, author.
Title: The crooked path to abolition : Abraham Lincoln
and the antislavery Constitution / James Oakes.
Description: First edition. | New York, N.Y. : W. W. Norton & Company, 2021. |
Includes bibliographical references and index.
Identifiers: LCCN 2020030366 | ISBN 9781324005858 (hardcover) |
ISBN 9781324005865 (epub)
Subjects: LCSH: Lincoln, Abraham, 1809–1865—Political and social views. |
Antislavery movements—United States—History—19th century. |
Slavery—Political aspects—United States—History—19th century. |
Constitutional history—United States.
Classification: LCC E449 .O1145 2021 | DDC 973.7/14—dc23
LC record available at https://lccn.loc.gov/2020030366

W. W. Norton & Company, Inc., 500 Fifth Avenue, New York, N.Y. 10110
www.wwnorton.com

W. W. Norton & Company Ltd., 15 Carlisle Street, London W1D 3BS

To my students,
with gratitude and admiration

Contents

Preface

IN EARLY 1861, on his long, meandering journey from Springfield, Illinois, to Washington, DC, president-elect Abraham Lincoln stopped in Philadelphia on February 21 and gave a couple of brief but revealing speeches. By then six slave states had seceded from the Union—a Union Lincoln was determined to hold together. At Independence Hall, inspired by the place where his country had been founded, Lincoln could "listen to those breathings rising within the consecrated walls where the Constitution of the United States, and, I will add, the Declaration of American Independence was originally framed." Lincoln believed that, taken together, these two documents—the Declaration and the Constitution—stated plainly the bedrock principles of the American nation. In one of those biblical allusions at which he was so adept, Lincoln swore an oath: "May my right hand forget its cunning and my tongue cleave to the roof of my mouth, if ever I prove false to those teachings."[1]

It was not "mere separation" from Great Britain that had inspired the revolutionary generation, Lincoln told his listeners that day in Philadelphia. They were aiming for something higher, "something in that Declaration giving liberty, not alone to the people of this country, but hope to the world for all future time. It was that which gave promise that in due time the weights should be lifted from the shoulders of all men, and that *all* should have an equal chance." This, Lincoln declared, "is the sentiment embodied in the Declaration of Independence." Now, as he faced the dismemberment of the Union, he wondered, "can this country be saved upon that basis?" If so, "I will consider myself one of the happiest men in the world." But what if the Union could only be preserved if Americans reneged on the promise of equality bequeathed by the founders? Standing in Independence Hall the soon-to-be president of the United States made one of the most startling statements of his career. "If this country cannot be saved without giving up that principle," Lincoln declared, "I would rather be assassinated on this spot."[2]

As unflinching as it was, Lincoln's firm commitment to fundamental human equality did not make him an abolitionist. He never called for the immediate emancipation of the slaves, the way most abolitionists did. He never denounced slaveholders as sinners and never endorsed the civil or political equality of Blacks and whites. He never claimed, as some abolitionists did, that the Constitution empowered Congress to abolish slavery in the states, nor did he agree with other abolitionists that the Constitution was a proslavery document. He never opened his home to fugitive slaves on the underground railroad. He endorsed the voluntary colonization of free Blacks long after most abolitionists had repudiated colonization outright. He never joined an abolitionist society, but he did join the Springfield branch of the American Colonization Society. He certainly spoke at colonization meetings and temperance meetings, but never at an abolitionist meeting. Lincoln supported due process rights for fugitive slaves, but he never endorsed outright defiance of the Fugitive Slave Act of 1850 and never denounced it as unconstitutional. Where abolitionists often publicized slavery's most gruesome features—the whippings, the sexual abuse, the brutal destruction of slave families—Lincoln rarely referred to such things. He was repelled by what he saw as the stridency of so much abolitionist rhetoric. As Eric Foner has said, Abraham Lincoln was not an abolitionist and never claimed to be.

But Lincoln always hated slavery as much, he once said, as any abolitionist. Like the abolitionists, Lincoln openly attacked slavery as a social, political, and moral evil. If there were differences between antislavery radicals and antislavery politicians like Lincoln, there were also substantial overlaps between them. Most abolitionists understood that in the end the problem of slavery required a political solution, and so they quite often framed their arguments in careful legal and constitutional terms—terms they generally shared with antislavery politicians. Like Lincoln and the Republicans, abolitionists considered themselves the heirs of the founders, the generation that had set in motion the abolition of slavery in the various states. Abolitionists worked hard, and with remarkable success, to formulate what I call the Antislavery Project, an agenda, a series of specific policies that were designed to stop and then reverse the expansion of slavery, policies that would—as Lincoln later explained—put slavery on "a course of ultimate extinction." By the 1850s abolitionists had succeeded in restoring the problem of slavery to the heart of American politics. They were now part of a vast and increasingly powerful antislavery movement, a coalition that embraced the majority of northern voters. That coalition, known as the Republican Party, constituted the left wing of the American political spectrum, and its most successful spokesman turned out to be Abraham Lincoln.

He was certainly much closer to the left than to the right. Conservatives disputed Lincoln's reading of the Declaration of Independence and often denied that it was linked to the Constitution. By the 1850s defenders of slavery not only distinguished the two documents but sometimes went so far as to dismiss entirely the principle of fundamental human equality. Northern Democrats who were indifferent to slavery, led by Illinois senator Stephen Douglas, read "all men are created equal" as "all *white* men are created equal." But for abolitionists, Republicans, and Lincoln, the Declaration meant everybody—men and women, Black and white. It meant that, at the very least, everybody was entitled to be free. It also meant that the promise of universal freedom was embodied in the Constitution.

Early in the twentieth century historians began to argue that there was a vast gulf between the soaring ideal of human equality so eloquently proclaimed in the Declaration of Independence and what they believed was the more conservative, elitist Constitution. Even today historians disagree about whether the principle of fundamental human equality represented a revolutionary new ideal or a hypocritical fantasy in a society that tolerated slavery. Are the inspiring sentiments of the Declaration's opening passages belied by a Constitution that recognized and protected human bondage? For the majority of northerners living in the middle of the nineteenth century, most of whom disliked slavery, the answer was no. Parse every clause of the Constitution, peer into the minds of its authors, and you may never find the antislavery document revered by so many ordinary men and women, Black and white, all across the North. But like the slaves who preferred the Book of Exodus to the epistles of St. Paul, or the radicalized British workers who had their own notions about the rights of Englishmen, northern farmers and artisans gave their allegiance to a Constitution that was unrecognizable to the Slave Power. Theirs was a popular constitutionalism—though not lacking for hefty scholarship—and millions of its adherents elected one of their own as president in 1860.

Lincoln once likened the Declaration to a picture, the Constitution to its frame. For him, as for most antislavery politicians, the men who drafted America's founding charter in the long summer of 1787 had committed the new nation to the principle of fundamental human equality. Fifty years later the great abolitionist William Lloyd Garrison would burn the Constitution in public, vehemently denouncing it as a covenant with Satan, a proslavery atrocity. But the majority of abolitionists didn't believe that, no antislavery politician believed that, and neither Abraham Lincoln nor the

people who voted for him believed it. For him—for them—
the Constitution was an antislavery document.

Why, Lincoln once asked, did "those old men, about the
time of the adoption of the Constitution," decree that slavery
should not go into new territories where it did not yet exist?
Why did they declare "that within twenty years the African
Slave Trade, by which slaves are supplied, might be cut off
by Congress?" What were these and other acts "but a clear
indication that the framers of the Constitution intended and
expected the ultimate extinction of the institution"?[3] For
Lincoln the antislavery Constitution made itself felt by its
practical consequences, by the various "acts" of the founders
and the justification for similar "acts" undertaken by their
descendants. Even in our own day politicians commonly
claim that the policies they advocate are grounded in the
Constitution.

But Lincoln lived in an age of "constitutionalism," as the
scholars call it, when every major issue was debated in constitutional terms. Was the treaty for the purchase of Louisiana
constitutionally sound? Was the Bank of the United States
constitutional? Could the federal government constitutionally support "internal improvements," what we would call
infrastructure projects? No other issue provoked as much
protracted constitutional wrangling as slavery. What power
did the Constitution give Congress to regulate slavery in the
territories? Did Congress have the constitutional authority to
abolish slavery in the District of Columbia? Did the fugitive
slave clause of the Constitution grant slaveholders a broad
right of property or a narrower "right of recaption"? Did

the Constitution grant "extraterritorial" protection to masters wherever they went with their slaves? Or did slaves who stepped outside the limits of a slave state instantly acquire the "privileges and immunities" guaranteed by the Constitution? And what, exactly, were those privileges and immunities?

When the Constitution was ratified, nearly everyone agreed that Congress had no power to "interfere" with—that is, abolish—slavery in a state. This had been true under the Articles of Confederation and it continued to be true under the Constitution. Historians call this the federal consensus. But the same principle protected *abolition* in the states: Congress had no power to interfere with emancipation in states that had established the presumption of freedom. This, too, raised a number of contentious constitutional questions. Could a state where freedom was presumed guarantee the rights of due process to men and women accused of being fugitive slaves? Did masters forfeit their slave property when they voluntarily carried their slaves into northern states that presumed freedom? And how far did that presumption of freedom extend? Did slavery follow the Constitution when southern masters migrated westward, or was freedom the "normal condition" of the territories? Did slaves acquire constitutional rights in US territorial waters?

Over time it became increasingly common for slaveholders to threaten secession if the northern states continued to deny southern masters the rights they believed were constitutionally protected. But threats of disunion only succeeded in raising another series of explosive constitutional questions. If a state seceded from the Union would its masters forfeit their constitutional right to recapture their fugitive slaves? If states where slaves were defined as moveable property went to war with the Union could federal armies constitutionally confiscate that property as "contraband of war"? Could President Lincoln, acting on his constitutional war powers, emancipate confiscated slaves? Indeed, was the Emancipation Proclamation unconstitutional?

Abolitionists developed compelling answers to all these questions. They narrowed down and sequestered the fugitive slave clause, deeming it a singular, limited exception to the general constitutional rule of freedom. They colonized various clauses of the Constitution—the Preamble, the privileges and immunities clause, the Fourth, Fifth, and Tenth amendments—for antislavery purposes. And from this antislavery Constitution they developed the Antislavery Project. Even abolitionists agreed that the federal government could not abolish slavery in a state, but it could suppress the slave trade, protect the rights of fugitive slaves, abolish slavery in Washington, DC, ban slavery from the western territories, and deny admission of new slave states into the Union. Such policies were made possible by the antislavery Constitution— the one Lincoln believed was created by the founders.

But something had gone wrong. Somewhere along the way a "Slave Power" had wrested control of the federal government and thrown the nation off its ordained course. The intellectual depth and popularity of antislavery constitutionalism were no match for the disproportionate power exercised by slaveholders in Congress, the presidency, and the Supreme Court. The goal of antislavery politics was to defeat this Slave Power and put the federal government back on the right track, to adopt policies that would, as the abolitionist William Jay put it in 1839, "ultimately exterminate" slavery. By the 1850s antislavery politicians were using the same language. Thaddeus Stevens called for the "final extinction" of slavery, and William Seward its "ultimate extinguishment." Lincoln would put slavery "on a course of ultimate extinction." That, they all argued, was what the founders intended.

At some point in the decades-long debate over slavery, every side claimed to be faithful to the intentions of the singular group of men they called the "founders." Who were these people? If in the 1780s the state legislators in Pennsylvania, New York, Connecticut, and Rhode Island qualified as founders, we can say that a majority of them clearly intended to put slavery on a course of ultimate extinction. But the same could hardly be said for their counterparts in the legislatures of Georgia and the Carolinas. The ambiguity remains if the founders include only the delegates at the 1787 Constitutional Convention. No doubt *some* of those men intended to perpetuate slavery and some intended, or at the very least expected, slavery to die. When it comes to the problem of slavery, as with many other issues great and small, it is simply not possible to discern a unified group of founders whose intentions can be readily discerned.[4]

That didn't stop people—years after the Constitutional Convention adjourned, in the heat of national debates over slavery—from ascribing implausible intentions to the founders. When the proslavery senator John C. Calhoun claimed that they intended to maintain an equilibrium between slave and free states, he was making it up. So was Supreme Court Justice Roger B. Taney when he asserted, as a truth too plain to be disputed, that the founders expressly recognized a constitutional right of property in slaves. They did no such thing. But Lincoln was also stretching it when he said that the founders intended to put slavery on a course of ultimate extinction. Some did and some didn't.

It may be that the intentions of those who produced the Constitution are irrelevant. It may be that what matters is the original meaning of the text itself. Distinguished legal scholars whose job it is to interpret the text have given us ingenious, even brilliant, but alas very different readings of what the Constitution actually says about slavery. It's not that the text is irrelevant. It matters that there was a fugitive slave clause and a three-fifths clause in the Constitution. Scholars disagree about how much those clauses mattered, but no one denies that they did. Indeed, together those two clauses might well be considered the bricks and mortar of the proslavery Constitution. The one guaranteed southern slaveholders the constitutional right to recapture slaves who escaped to states where slavery was abolished or was being abolished. But there was tremendous dispute between northerners and southerners over exactly what sort of "rights" the fugitive slave clause created, who should enforce them, and how they should be enforced.

The three-fifths clause was no less proslavery, and its consequences were substantial. If it is not entirely clear whether one or two slaveholders were elected president by virtue of the South's increased influence in the Electoral College, there is little doubt that the three-fifths clause gave the slave states enough extra votes in the House of Representatives to alter the outcome of the Missouri Crisis and to secure the passage of the Indian Removal Act, the Fugitive Slave Act of 1850, and the Kansas-Nebraska Act of 1854. Here was the proslavery Constitution, and it mattered. To be sure, these proslavery victories always required the votes of a minority of northern senators and representatives. If it was never sufficient to sustain the federal power of the slaveholders, the three-fifths clause was always necessary.

But there was also an antislavery Constitution and it, too, mattered. Congress was granted the power to make "all needful rules and regulations" for the territories, and for decades after ratification hardly anyone doubted that this authorized the federal government to ban slavery from the territories. Excise that right from the text and it's hard to imagine the restrictions on slavery in the Northwest Territory and the bulk of the Louisiana Purchase, the protracted debate over the so-called Wilmot Proviso that would ban slavery from the Mexican cession, or the violent response to the Kansas-Nebraska Act. In fact, without the territorial clause it's hard to imagine the Republican Party. Similarly, the exclusive legislation clause gave Congress the power to abolish slavery and the slave trade in Washington, DC. That constitutional power was another source of contention between slave states and free states.

Then there was the familiar assertion that the principle of fundamental human equality was embodied in the Constitution. The text itself proved the point—or so slavery's opponents believed. Doesn't the Preamble state that the purpose of the federal government was to "secure the blessings of liberty," and wasn't liberty one of those natural rights to which everyone was equally entitled? Similarly, the Fifth

Amendment declares that "no person" could be deprived of life, liberty, or property without due process of law. How is that different from saying that "all men" are equally entitled to "Life, Liberty and the pursuit of Happiness"? At the very least it was a plausible inference, based on the text, that the principle of fundamental human equality was "embodied" in the Constitution.

As with the territorial clause, it's hard to imagine antislavery politics without the due process clause. The fact that the fugitive slave clause was located in Article IV implied that the states could require due process rights for accused fugitives, which the northern states immediately proceeded to do—to the consternation of the slave states. By the 1830s opponents of slavery increasingly invoked the Fifth Amendment to claim that accused fugitive slaves were entitled to their day in court. By the 1850s it was a commonplace of antislavery politics that Congress would actually violate the Fifth Amendment if it so much as allowed slavery into the territories.

Taken together these various clauses added up to the antislavery Constitution, based on the text, and hardly the figment of the antislavery imagination. Long before the Civil War, antislavery constitutionalism was the conventional wisdom among millions of northerners, not to mention a majority of the northern representatives in Congress.

And yet when the Constitution was ratified there was no such thing as proslavery or antislavery constitutionalism. Both developed over time, and by 1820 the two competing interpretations of the Constitution were substantially elaborated during the protracted debates over the admission of Missouri to statehood. It is a mistake, then, to think of the proslavery Constitution as original and the antislavery Constitution as a latter-day invention. The two Constitutions emerged in reaction to each other, and they continued to develop through the last decades of the antebellum era, each side solemnly invoking the text produced by the founders.

But the text will take us only so far. Throughout the decades-long debate over slavery and the Constitution some of the most contentious issues arose over constitutional principles that cannot be found in the actual wording of the Constitution. Nowhere does the Constitution state that Congress cannot "interfere" with slavery or abolition in a state, yet it was widely agreed that it could not. Nor does the Constitution expressly recognize a right of "property in man," notwithstanding the later assertion by Justice Taney that it does. These two particular *absences* profoundly shaped the debates over slavery and the Constitution, despite the fact that they refer to principles that are nowhere to be found in the text.

Given that the Constitution was the handiwork of men who disagreed about slavery, it is hardly surprising that it could be—and was—read as both proslavery and antislavery. Even today scholars disagree over whether the compromises of 1787 produced a Constitution that was fundamentally proslavery.[5] My own view is that, depending on which clauses you cite and how you spin them, the Constitution can be read as either proslavery or antislavery. And yet scholarly debates over slavery in the Constitution tend toward the tendentious. It has been argued, for example, that antislavery constitutionalists underestimated the significance of the Constitution's proslavery clauses, that they saw ambiguity where there was really no ambiguity to be found. William Lloyd Garrison and John C. Calhoun were right after all: There was a single "original meaning"—clearly, powerfully proslavery— embedded in the text of the Constitution itself. If so, the defenders of freedom, however well-intentioned, were sadly mistaken to indulge the illusion that the Constitution was an antislavery document.

But antislavery constitutionalists replied that their opponents went beyond tendentiousness, that proslavery constitutionalists flat out made things up. *They* read an "express" right of "property in man" into a Constitution that contained no such right. *They* made the preposterous claim that the Declaration of Independence proclaimed the equality of states rather than people. *They* claimed, implausibly, that Congress had no constitutional authority to abolish slavery in Washington, DC, or to ban slavery from the territories. *They* claimed, on no textual basis whatsoever, that slavery followed the Constitution onto the high seas, into the territories, and even into the free states of the North. Were they right?

Once upon a time a firm yes or no answer would have come easily to me, but I now think it's a mistake to dismiss antislavery constitutionalism too readily. No doubt there was a proslavery Constitution and an antislavery Constitution; both were grounded in the text, in inferences drawn from the text, in legal premises and racial ideologies beyond the text, and in the diverse intentions of the founders who wrote it. But the antislavery reading now strikes me as more compelling—and the proslavery reading less persuasive— than I once believed.

Clouding the issue is the fact that the question between them was not simply *Who got the Constitution right?* but who had the power to enforce one version of the Constitution over the other. In the early years of the republic the slave states enjoyed the disproportionate political power that flowed from having the largest populations and the richest economies. But as the decades passed, the northern economy proved more dynamic; its growing cities, its burgeoning factories, and its prosperous farms attracted millions of immigrant workers, and by the 1850s the balance of political power was noticeably shifting from the slave South to the free states. In a counterpoint familiar to all historians of the sectional crisis, antislavery constitutionalists became increasingly aggressive as proslavery constitutionalists made increasingly extreme demands for federal protection of slavery.

LIKE INTERPRETATIONS OF the Constitution, Lincoln's popular reputation tends toward the tendentious. He was either the Great Emancipator, a secular saint, the man who freed millions of slaves with the stroke of his pen. Or he was a reluctant emancipator, an instinctive conservative whose willingness to attack slavery was held in check by his inability to imagine that Black people, once freed, could live as equals among white Americans. Both versions of Lincoln assume he had enormous powers that he simply did not have. He did not free all the slaves with the stroke of his pen because he could not. The idea that he could may be a function of the times we live in. After a succession of "imperial" presidents, it is sometimes hard to remember that Lincoln lived in a world where the Constitution limited at least as much as it empowered.[6]

Here I propose a third Lincoln, one whose commitment

to the federal consensus, far more than white supremacy, accounts for his deliberate approach to emancipation and abolition. For antislavery constitutionalism was in many ways a doctrine of restraint. Abolitionists repeatedly claimed that the federal government had stepped beyond its constitutional authority—when it admitted Florida and Arkansas to the Union as slave states, legalized slavery in Washington, DC, authorized fugitive slave renditions without due process, deployed US troops to assist slaveholders in the recapture of fugitive slaves, or demanded the return of slaves who rebelled on the high seas. When antislavery radicals called on the federal government to "divorce" itself from slavery or insisted on a "strict construction" of the fugitive slave clause, they did so on the ground that the Constitution should have restrained the government from pursuing a host of proslavery policies. But the opponents of slavery were likewise constrained by the federal consensus. Whatever else the federal government could do, the one thing nearly everyone agreed it could not do was abolish slavery in a state.

However, constitutional restraint did not mean constitutional impotence. Quite the contrary. At the very least the antislavery Constitution empowered the federal government to abolish the Atlantic slave trade, ban slavery from the territories, abolish slavery in Washington, DC, protect the due process rights of fugitive slaves, deny admission to new slave states, and emancipate slaves in wartime. By some lights the Constitution authorized the federal government to suppress the domestic slave trade, or at least the coastwise slave trade, and acknowledge the rights of slave rebels on the high seas. In the context of civil war, antislavery constitutionalism provided the legal basis for the single most revolutionary moment in the political history of the United States: the liberation of four million enslaved Americans.

It is therefore crucial to understand how, over the course of his career, Abraham Lincoln came to endorse the same basic principles of antislavery constitutionalism embraced by most abolitionists. He denied that the Constitution protected slavery as a right of property. He claimed that all slaves brought into the territories were presumptively free. Slaves who stepped beyond the borders of a slave state were thereby entitled to the rights of due process, the privileges and immunities of citizens, and the right against arbitrary seizure. In 1860 the platform on which Lincoln was elected president went far beyond claiming that Congress should ban slavery in the territories; it denied that Congress could constitutionally *allow* a territorial legislature to legalize slavery. That same platform rehearsed the most vital precept of antislavery constitutionalism—that the egalitarian principles of the Declaration of Independence were "embodied" in the US Constitution. For Lincoln, who repeatedly claimed that the promise of fundamental human equality was flatly incompatible with slavery, the conclusion was inescapable: Despite a couple of carefully delimited rights guaranteed to the slaveholders, the Constitution itself was an antislavery document. In the phraseology of his day, the Constitution made freedom the rule and slavery the exception.

Having adopted the major precepts of antislavery constitutionalism, it is hardly surprising that Lincoln would also embrace the various policies specified in the Antislavery Project—a project first enunciated by abolitionists in the 1820s and 1830s. As a young member of the Illinois state legislature Lincoln issued a public statement declaring that Congress could, "under the Constitution," abolish slavery in Washington, DC, and a decade later he drafted legislation for Congress to do so. In the 1840s, as a member of the US House of Representatives, Lincoln voted repeatedly to ban slavery from all the western territories. In the 1850s he called for revisions of the Fugitive Slave Act that would guarantee due process to those accused of running away and demanded more aggressive suppression of slavery on the high seas. By the end of the decade, with threats of secession swirling about, Lincoln warned that if the slave states seceded they would forfeit their constitutional right to recapture their fugitive slaves, a warning he repeated in his inaugural address.

Lincoln made good on that last threat within weeks of the outbreak of war by endorsing the action of US Army generals who refused to return "contraband" slaves to their masters. In August of 1861, after Congress authorized the permanent forfeiture of contrabands, Lincoln acted on his constitutional powers as commander in chief to emancipate contrabands on the grounds of "military necessity."

The threat of the Antislavery Project was significant enough to cause the slave states to secede, hurling the nation into a bloody civil war. But precisely because there was a war there's no way to know whether the project would have worked in peacetime. It is, however, reasonably certain that the Civil War would not have led to the destruction of slavery in the absence of the antislavery Constitution. One of the many continuities between antislavery constitutional theory and wartime practice lies in Lincoln's approach to fugitive slaves. It's not hard to see the connection between the constitutional claim that slaves were presumed free when they set foot on free soil and the Union policy of freeing slaves who set foot within Union lines where the Constitution overrode state and local laws establishing slavery. For enslaved men and women, federal policy vested the often-solitary act of running away with tremendous political significance. After Fort Sumter, the constitutional precepts of peacetime became the revolutionary weapons of wartime.

As president Lincoln made it his administration's policy not to return the fugitives of disloyal owners within weeks after the Civil War began. A few months later he declared "contraband" slaves emancipated. Three months after that he drafted an abolition statute that was a model for the four slave states that remained in the Union. From those beginnings his antislavery policy became steadily more radical. In the first half of 1862 he signed off on a raft of congressional bills that implemented the Antislavery Project. Those laws made it a crime for anyone in the US military to participate in the capture and return of fugitive slaves, abolished slavery in Washington, DC, required West Virginia to abolish slavery as a condition for admission to the Union, and banned slavery from the western territories. In his first year as president Lincoln negotiated the treaty with Great Britain that led, within a few years, to the end of the 350-year-old Atlantic slave trade.

As the crisis moved into its second year federal antislavery policy became more and more aggressive until, with the Emancipation Proclamation, war became revolution. In the early months of 1862 Lincoln began to warn the loyal states that *emancipation* would soon lead to *abolition*. His famous proclamation of January 1, 1863, declared emancipation universal in all the disloyal parts of the South, and in the middle of that year Lincoln began using emancipation to weaken slavery in all the southern states until, one by one, they began to abolish slavery on their own. This was the original goal of the abolitionists—federal encouragement of state abolition—now radicalized by war. So much so that by January 1865 there were enough free states to make ratification of the Thirteenth Amendment possible. Had they not done so, it is doubtful the Thirteenth Amendment abolishing slavery nationwide could have succeeded.

THERE ARE THOUSANDS of books about Abraham Lincoln and dozens of them on the sixteenth president's supposedly conservative commitment to, or scandalous violations of, the Constitution. But only a few place his antislavery politics within the context of his antislavery constitutionalism, largely because we lack a comprehensive history of the antislavery Constitution to which Lincoln was devoted. As I began digging into that history my own thinking evolved. Where I once contrasted Lincoln the pragmatic politician with Frederick Douglass the principled abolitionist, it now seems to me that by 1860 their views of the Constitution, though different, nevertheless had more in common than I once thought. I now suspect that Lincoln's evolving views on racial equality were closely tied to his deepening commitment to antislavery constitutionalism. The continuities I once vaguely discerned between the antislavery politics of the pre–Civil War decades and the wartime destruction of slavery come into sharper focus when viewed through the lens of antislavery constitutionalism. Through that same lens—the antislavery Constitution—Lincoln's commitment to the Union and his hostility to slavery become indistinguishable. Slave resistance has long been central to my thinking about the Civil War era, but only in recent years has it become clear to me that an antislavery Constitution created openings for fugitive slaves that a proslavery Constitution would have foreclosed. In short, I have become convinced that a full understanding of antislavery constitutionalism is necessary for a full understanding of the origins of the single most important achievement of Abraham Lincoln's presidency: the restoration of the Union by means of the revolutionary overthrow of the largest and wealthiest slave society on earth.

But it was a crooked path that led to abolition, with forks and byways that could easily have led to dead ends, or to a very different end. If the outcome was hardly inevitable, however, neither was it accidental. The revolution happened in the same space all humans occupy, that vast netherworld between determinism and free will, between "structure" and "contingency," the place where people make their own history but not on their own terms. Lincoln entered the presidency having sworn to uphold the Constitution and restore the Union, but not just any Constitution and not just any Union. With each new twist of fate, with every unexpected turn of events—the military setbacks, the political challenges, the diplomatic scares—Lincoln responded in ways consistent with his long-standing commitment to an antislavery Constitution and the more perfect Union—the antislavery Union—he believed the founders intended to establish. As war became revolution, ultimate extinction became unconditional abolition, a "fundamental and astounding" turn of events, Lincoln mused, but a turn that had its origins in his determination—and the determination of hundreds of thousands—to restore a Union founded on the great principle of fundamental human equality. If he had to do it any other way, he said, he would rather be assassinated.

⇜ 1 ⇝

"That Glorious Fabric of Collected Wisdom"

A Brief History of the Antislavery Constitution

We hold this truth to be self-evident, that God created all men equal, is one of the most prominent features in the Declaration of Independence, and in that glorious fabric of collected wisdom, our noble Constitution.[1]

James Forten, 1813

In the discussion of political subjects, we shall ever regard the constitution of the United States as our polar star.[2]

Samuel E. Cornish and John B. Russwurm, 1827

IN JULY 1848, frustrated by Congress's inability to agree on what to do about slavery in the territories, Delaware senator John Clayton proposed a compromise. Congress, he thought, should stay out of the issue entirely and allow the status of slavery in the territories "to be settled by the silent operation of the Constitution itself." If an issue over slavery arose within the territories, Clayton proposed, let

the Supreme Court decide what the Constitution decreed.
John Hale, the intrepid antislavery senator from New Hampshire, thought Clayton's idea was ridiculous. The Constitution did not speak with one voice on slavery, Hale noted. It "was interpreted as variously as the Bible." John C. Calhoun, the proslavery senator from South Carolina, "was for leaving the matter to the Constitution," Hale pointed out, "because, in his opinion, the Constitution carries slavery with it." But a different senator from a free state "construes the Constitution as meaning to secure freedom. The client of the Senator from Vermont asks how is this settled?"

"Oh by the Constitution!"

"Well, that is very well, but what does the Constitution say?"

"Oh, it is a Constitution of freedom."

"Very well, I am satisfied, as freedom is what I want."

"In the South, the same question is asked, and the citizen there is satisfied because he is told that it carries slavery with it."[3]

In 1860 Abraham Lincoln ran for president on a Republican Party platform that proved Hale's point by repeatedly invoking a Constitution that favored freedom over slavery. It proclaimed freedom to be the "normal condition of all the territory of the United States." The Republicans did not directly call on Congress to pass a law banning slavery from the territories. What they actually said was that Congress had no authority "to give legal existence to slavery in any territory of the United States." It wasn't that Congress lacked the power to ban slavery, it was that Congress had no constitutional power to *allow* slavery into the territories. Natural law decreed that all human beings were born free, and the Constitution affirmed that principle. Its Preamble secured "the promise of liberty to ourselves and our posterity." The Fifth Amendment decreed that no person could be deprived of liberty without due process of law. Congress could, if need be, pass laws protecting the freedoms of all those residing in the territories, but it could not pass a law establishing slavery nor could it allow a territorial legislature to do so. So freedom was more than the normal condition of the territories, it was the constitutionally protected condition of the territories. That's because the Constitution—the Constitution as Lincoln and the Republicans understood it—was an antislavery document. To be sure, the founders had made compromises with slavery in order to create the Union, but those proslavery clauses were exceptions in a Constitution whose general rule was freedom. This was antislavery constitutionalism, and it saturated the Republican Party platforms of 1856 as well as 1860.

Both platforms asserted that the principles of fundamental human equality and universal liberty "promulgated" in the Declaration of Independence were literally "embodied in the Constitution." Debates over the meaning of the Declaration were commonplace in 1860, and the antislavery meaning had a potent ideological sting. Anybody who followed antislavery politics would have recognized what the Republicans were saying: If the promise of universal freedom was "embodied in the Constitution," it followed that the Constitution was imbued with an antislavery spirit. That spirit could be suppressed by "positive" laws, basically statutes, within the slave states. But unlike the states, the territories were under the direct sovereign authority of a Constitution whose basic rule was freedom. Once a state was created and admitted to the Union it could legalize slavery, but Congress could never do that. Congress could only pass laws to protect the freedom of everyone in the territories.

There was more. Because everyone in the territories was presumed to be free, all were entitled to the protections afforded by the Fifth Amendment. As the 1860 platform put it, "our Republican fathers, when they had abolished slavery in all our national territory, ordained that 'no person shall be deprived of life, liberty or property without due process of law.'" This was no newfangled doctrine. As far back as the 1640s English radicals drew antislavery inferences from the rights of due process. In the absence of a positive law creating slavery, it was said, habeas corpus liberates the slave. This was the premise of Lord Mansfield's influential decision in the *Somerset* ruling of 1772. Slavery was such an "odious" violation of natural law, Mansfield declared, that it required a positive law to override the presumption of freedom. In the absence of such a statute anyone in England who was being held as a slave could sue for freedom on a writ of habeas corpus. The Republican Party invoked that same premise when it quoted the due process clause of the Constitution in the 1860 platform. A slave who was carried into federal territory was entitled to "due process of law." The slave could actually sue the putative owner for freedom on a writ of habeas corpus, and the owner, unable to cite a territorial or congressional statute justifying the claim of property in the slave, forfeited the claim. The slave, having set foot on free soil, was thereby emancipated.

The 1860 platform went still further. According to the Republicans, the Constitution did not merely *allow* Congress to protect the Fifth Amendment rights of everyone in federal territory, it *obligated* Congress to ensure that no person was deprived of their liberty without due process of law. It is "our duty," the Republicans proclaimed, "by legislation, whenever such legislation is necessary, to maintain this provision of the Constitution." Hence the conclusion: If Congress was obliged to protect the freedom of all persons in the territories, it followed that Congress could not, constitutionally, "give legal existence to slavery in any territory of the United States." "The Constitution contains no power to make a King or to support kingly rule," Massachusetts senator Charles Sumner explained in 1852. "With similar reason it may be said, that it contains no power to make a slave or to support a system of slavery."[4] This was a sentiment familiar to all antislavery politicians.

Defenders of slavery, led by the chief justice of the US Supreme Court, claimed that the Constitution "expressly" recognized slaves as "property." Republicans vehemently rejected this. Their 1860 party platform denied that "the personal relations between master and servant . . . involve an unqualified property in persons." Property rights in human beings represented "a purely local interest," Republicans declared, an "interest" that existed only in the southern states where slavery was still legal. This, too, was familiar antislavery dogma. No abolitionist would have denied that slaves were legally property, made so by the positive laws of the southern states. But antislavery constitutionalists pointed out that the Constitution deliberately referred to slaves as "persons."

They were "property" by a mere "legal" right, a right that existed only within the boundaries of the slave states.

Proslavery constitutionalists reversed this logic. Of course they cited those parts of the Constitution that explicitly recognized slavery, notably the three-fifths and the fugitive slave clauses. What those clauses actually did, they claimed, was recognize slavery as a constitutionally protected right of property—a right that was prior to and "higher" than the Constitution but that was also embodied in the document itself. In the proslavery reading of the Constitution the Fifth Amendment guaranteed not the liberty of the slave but the property right of the master. All forms of property were legally created by the states and slave property was no different, proslavery constitutionalists argued, and the Constitution protected every "species of property" in exactly the same way. Slavery's defenders insisted that Congress had no power to deprive anyone of their constitutional right to bring slave property into the territories. Indeed, so powerful was the right of "property in man" that Congress was constitutionally incapable of abolishing slavery in Washington, DC. By 1860 proslavery politicians would argue that Congress had a constitutional obligation to protect slave property in the territories. They especially cited the fugitive slave clause as proof that the founders had gone out of their way to protect slavery as a constitutional right of property, and this further obligated Congress to enforce that right within the free states of the North, over and against the laws of those states and the will of their people.

The property right was the linchpin of the slavery debate. If slaves were property under the Constitution, neither the rights of persons nor the privileges and immunities of citizenship applied to them. As a constitutionally protected "species of property," slaves had no access to the various civil protections they might have claimed as constitutionally recognized "persons." When seven slave states seceded from the Union in the wake of Lincoln's election, six of them met in Montgomery, Alabama, in early 1861 to draft a Confederate constitution that nearly duplicated the US Constitution. The Confederates reproduced the three-fifths and fugitive slave clauses as well as the ban on the importation of slaves. They also duplicated all the clauses cited by antislavery constitutionalists—the Preamble, the due process clause, and the privileges and immunities clauses. The one conspicuous change, however, was that the Confederate constitution explicitly referred to slaves as "property" and protected slave property as a constitutional right. That changed everything, because it meant that the various promises and protections of rights and freedom did not apply to slaves.

By contrast, Abraham Lincoln, like nearly all opponents of slavery, assumed that because the US Constitution referred to slaves as "persons" rather than property, enslaved men and women were entitled to at least some of the rights, privileges, and immunities guaranteed to all persons whenever they stepped beyond the borders of the slave states themselves—in the territories, the free states, or on the high seas. The denial of the property right was a central theme of Lincoln's last major antislavery speech, at the Cooper Institute in New York City, on February 27, 1860. The southerners allude "to an assumed Constitutional right of yours, to take slaves into the federal territories, and to hold them there as property," Lincoln said. "But no such right is specifically written in the Constitution. That instrument is literally silent about any such right. We, on the contrary, deny that such a right has any existence in the Constitution, even by implication."[5] The critical absence of a constitutional right of "property in man" was another foundational precept among those who opposed slavery.

Here was the irreconcilable conflict between slavery and freedom, framed in constitutional terms, openly announced in the competing platforms of the northern Republican and southern Democratic parties in 1860.[6] Of the four major candidates who campaigned for the presidency that year, Lincoln stood out as the only one running on a platform grounded on the principles of antislavery constitutionalism. None of the others invoked the Declaration of Independence, much less claimed that the principle of fundamental human equality was embodied in the Constitution. None denied, as Republicans did, that there was a constitutional right of "property in man." None but the Republicans cited the Fifth Amendment guarantee of liberty. Certainly no other platform decreed that Congress was constitutionally obligated to protect the due process rights of all persons in the territories, including what the Constitution termed "persons held to service." And no other party claimed that Congress was constitutionally prohibited from allowing slavery into the territories.

It is impossible to appreciate the serious implications of Lincoln's election in 1860 without understanding that the Republican Party platform on which he ran represented a potent distillation of an antislavery constitutional tradition that originated in the famous compromises between slavery and freedom that were hammered out at the Constitutional Convention at Philadelphia in 1787.

-»»)«««-

AT FIRST there was nothing to compromise. On July 4, 1776, thirteen slave colonies declared themselves an independent nation composed of thirteen slave states. Some of those colonies had passed laws banning the slave trade, and many Americans viewed the ban as a first step toward the abolition of slavery itself. In 1774 Rhode Island actually passed an abolition statute. But such colonial statutes were uniformly disallowed or disregarded by imperial authorities in Britain, where an antislavery movement was yet to be born. This meant that in creating a new nation there was no need for slave states to compromise with free states, because there were no free states.

Eleven years later the situation had changed dramatically. The slave states were still the largest, wealthiest, and most politically powerful in the new nation. Yet when the delegates met in Philadelphia to draft a new constitution, several states—Pennsylvania, Rhode Island, and Connecticut—had passed abolition statutes. Massachusetts had outlawed slavery judicially. Both houses of the New York assembly had approved an abolition statute, though it was subsequently overruled by the state's archaic Council of Revision. Vermont, soon to join the United States, had set abolition in motion in its 1777 constitution. One by one individual states were abolishing slavery, and the accumulation of those states came to be known as the North.

This was a revolutionary departure after centuries—millennia, really—in which slavery had been accepted as perfectly legal throughout most of the world. Though slavery had disappeared from much of northern and western Europe in the Middle Ages, it was spectacularly revived with the European colonization of the Americas beginning in the sixteenth century. By 1787 slavery had roots in North American soil that were more than a century and a half old. To be sure, slavery had always had its critics, not least among the slaves, and the criticism became more trenchant even as slavery in the British colonies grew and flourished. But the outright abolition of slavery? That was a new and radical thing in the history of the world.[7] Yet there it was, an antislavery interest pressing its claims at the Constitutional Convention in Philadelphia in 1787. Unlike 1776, there were now free states and slave states meeting head-on, and if there was to be a unified nation there would have to be compromise. The Constitution, notoriously, was exactly that.

Numerous scholars have combed through the debates at the Constitutional Convention, filtering out the often-obscure processes by which the compromises between slavery and freedom were arrived at. But however byzantine or indecipherable the process, the results are not that hard to discern, and the important thing about them is that they tilt in both proslavery and antislavery directions. On the crucial matter of representation, antislavery delegates wanted slaves entirely excluded from the population count whereas defenders of slavery wanted to count all slaves for purposes of representation. Neither side got what it wanted. Instead, the compromise agreed to was the infamous three-fifths clause, which counted sixty percent of the slaves for purposes of representation in the lower house, as well as for purposes of direct federal taxation. The direct taxation provision was effectively irrelevant because Congress only imposed such taxes in a few emergencies,[8] but the representation clause gave the slave states added power in both the House of Representatives and the Electoral College.

The Constitution also incorporated the fugitive slave clause from the Ordinance of 1787, which banned slavery from the Northwest Territory. In a sense, the fugitive slave clause was the price opponents of slavery paid for the congressional right to ban slavery in the territories. Because it gave slaveholders a right they had always enjoyed—at least until the northern states began abolishing slavery—the fugitive slave clause was relatively uncontroversial at the time it was adopted. Together, the three-fifths and fugitive slave clauses are generally read, with good reason, as victories for the slave states, despite those states' failure to get all they wanted or things they did not already have.

However, the fugitive slave clause was critically ambiguous in ways that led to sharply differing interpretations. On the one hand, it vested slaveholders with a common-law "right of recaption," that is, the right of the owner to recover property or persons—wives, children, apprentices, servants—without any resort to legal process, so long as the recovery "be not in a riotous manner."[9] This was the right slaveholders relied on during the colonial period when recapturing runaway slaves. On the other hand, the fugitive slave clause was located in

Article IV, which regulates the relations among states or between states and the federal government. This made fugitive slave renditions a matter of "comity" between states without imposing any restrictions on a state's ability to regulate such renditions within its own borders.

In effect, the Constitution established two different legal approaches to fugitive slaves: the master's summary right of recaption, and the state's power to require due process in fugitive slave renditions. The result was conflict. Slaveholders would claim that the Constitution, in recognizing a right of recaption, necessarily recognized a right of property in a slave. (Actually, the common-law right of recaption applied to both property and persons, and the fugitive slave clause referred to runaway slaves as "persons.") Yet from the start northern states interpreted the clause as a recognition of their power to protect Black persons within their borders based on the presumption of freedom. Pennsylvania's 1780 gradual abolition statute granted slaves the same due process rights as white servants. In 1788, as soon as the Constitution was ratified, Pennsylvania amended its law to protect "any negro or mulatto, from any part or parts of this state," from being summarily carried out of the state as a slave. Slave catchers were thereby treated as kidnappers who, upon conviction, were subject to steep fines and up to twelve months in prison.[10] In the late 1780s most northern states passed similar laws protecting the due process rights of accused fugitives. Through their power to regulate fugitive slave renditions, northern states could come close to nullifying the slaveholder's constitutionally recognized right of recaption.

The slave trade clause was less ambiguous. Although it

was initially interpreted in different ways, it was ultimately a victory for slavery's opponents—despite their desire to ban the trade at an earlier date. At the Philadelphia convention the delegates from the Lower South initially threatened to walk out if the Constitution gave Congress any power at all to regulate the slave trade, including the power to tax slave imports. Clearly they relented. The Constitution empowered Congress to ban states from importing slaves beginning in 1808, to tax slave imports before that date, and to ban slave imports into US territory immediately. This was a major grant of federal power to deprive the states of their previously exclusive authority over the importation of slaves.

The Constitution also gave Congress the power to make "all needful rules and regulations" for the territories, including the power to ban slavery.[11] This power would also become a major source of tension between the slave and free states. Together Congress's power to ban slavery from the territories and to prohibit states from importing slaves—despite the delay—were victories for the antislavery delegates.

Other features of the constitutional settlement protected the interests of both the free and the slave states. Congress was prevented from imposing export duties, which benefitted the slave states whose livelihood depended on exportable staple crops. But Congress was simultaneously empowered to impose tariffs on imports, a power that was used to protect the nascent manufacturing interests of the Northeast—a source of enormous irritation to the slave states in later years. Other pieces of the constitutional fabric, though not directly speaking to slavery, provoked a number of prickly questions. Did the full faith and credit clause compel free

states to recognize the property rights of slave owners traveling in the North with their slaves? Or did it require the slave
states to recognize the citizenship rights of northern Blacks
working as seamen on merchant vessels docked in southern
ports? Did the Constitution compel antislavery northerners
to help suppress slave insurrections in the southern states, or
did it empower the federal government to emancipate slaves
in the very act of suppressing domestic insurrections? Did
the Fifth Amendment guarantee the master's right of property in a slave? Or did it ensure that no "person" could be
deprived of liberty without due process of law?

Such questions arose in large part because the text of
the Constitution always referred to slaves as "persons," never
as property. Scholars have drawn all manner of unsavory
inferences and shameful motives from the delegates' failure to come right out and use the word "slave" in a Constitution packed with direct and indirect references to slavery.[12]
Maybe. But it seems unreasonable to dismiss the antislavery
convictions of the delegates from the North who arrived in
Philadelphia from states where the legitimacy of "property
in man" had been recently and extensively debated. By 1787
opponents of slavery took it as a given that property in man
violated natural law, common law, and divine law.[13] They
were not inclined to legitimize it in constitutional law.

At the Philadelphia convention Roger Sherman of Connecticut, on two separate occasions, objected to a proposed
tax on slave imports "as acknowledging men to be property."
James Madison of Virginia agreed and shortly after the convention adjourned he inserted into his notes his own view
that it would be "wrong to admit in the Constitution the idea

that there could be property in men." The wording of the offending clause was changed to indicate that the proposed tax referred to slaves as "persons." Later in the convention Charles Cotesworth Pinckney, a wealthy South Carolina planter and one of the convention's most indefatigable defenders of slavery, complained about the wording of the proposed privileges and immunities clause. He "seemed to wish some provision should be included in favor of property in slaves," Madison noted. But the delegates brushed Pinckney's objection aside, and the expansively worded privileges and immunities clause in Article IV would later emerge as a centerpiece of antislavery constitutionalism. This was in large part because the text of the Constitution refers to slaves only as persons, never as property.[14]

The Constitution thus reaffirmed Congress's right to ban slavery from the territories *and* the slaveholders' right to recapture their fugitive slaves. It deliberately referred to slaves as "persons" rather than property, yet it preserved a right of recaption which the slaveholders took to imply a right of "property in man." It gave the southern states additional power in the lower house of Congress and enhanced influence in the election of presidents. But it gave Congress the power to regulate and ban the importation of slaves, a power that was previously the preserve of the states. A Constitution that sanctioned slavery in some ways and sanctioned antislavery in others could not help but give rise to conflicting interpretations, some of which were on display during the ratification debates in the states.

Neither the Federalists who supported ratification nor the Antifederalists who opposed it developed consistent arguments for or against the Constitution's treatment of slavery. Southern Antifederalists—especially in Virginia—vigorously denounced the Constitution as an existential threat to slavery, whereas southern Federalists fairly boasted of the Constitution's robust protections of slavery. In the North the opponents of slavery were divided as well. Though none thought the Constitution as a whole was either proslavery or antislavery, Antifederalists aimed their attacks on the slave trade and three-fifths clauses while antislavery Federalists defended both. As in the convention itself, there was hardly any discussion of the fugitive slave clause.[15]

Oddly, the debate over the three-fifths clause among northern opponents of slavery focused more on taxation than representation. In the proposed Constitution direct taxes would be based on population rather than on property values. Defenders of the clause claimed that this was beneficial to the North because northern farms were more valuable per acre. A tax based on land values would have benefitted the southern states because slave plantations had less "improved" acreage per capita. Critics claimed that northerners had more children and lived longer than southerners; direct taxation based on population was therefore biased against the North. But the debate turned out to be moot because the federal government rarely imposed direct taxes.

The debate over the representation clause was a bit more sophisticated. Northern Federalists who were opposed to slavery defended the three-fifths rule on the ground that representation based on population was more republican and less aristocratic than representation based on property. They invoked the classical economic critique of slavery, arguing that because slave labor was intrinsically less productive than free labor, it was appropriate to count only three-fifths of the slave population for purposes of representation. Antifederalists, citing Locke and Montesquieu, claimed that no slaves should be represented because they stood outside the political community. Some said that because slaves were property, they should not be counted at all. Nevertheless, the debate among antislavery northerners over slave representation was relatively muted during ratification, certainly compared to what it became in later years.

The slave trade clause was by far the most important source of division among northern opponents of slavery, despite the fact that both sides agreed that the slave trade was a monstrous evil. As a summary of the debate in Massachusetts explained: "Both sides deprecated the slave-trade in the most pointed terms." One side lamented the fact that "this constitution provided for the continuation of the slave trade for 20 years." The other side "rejoiced that a door was now opened, for the annihilation of this odious, abhorrent practice."[16] It was fairly common for opponents of slavery to view the prospective ban on slave imports as a harbinger of slavery's eventual demise.

During the ratification debates antislavery advocates often compared the Constitution's slave trade provision favorably to the Articles of Confederation. "Under the present confederation, the states may admit the importation of slaves as long as they please," James Wilson explained, but thanks to the slave trade article, "after the year 1808, the congress will have power to prohibit such importation, notwithstanding the disposition of any state to the contrary. I consider this as laying the foundation for banishing slavery out of this country."[17] Isaac Backus agreed. "In the articles of confederation, no provision was made to hinder the importation of slaves into any of these States," he explained, "but a door has now opened, hereafter to do it." Backus then repeated the familiar hope that, although slavery had not been destroyed in a single blow, "yet we may hope it will die with a consumption."[18] Because the Constitution gave Congress a power it lacked under the Articles of Confederation, antislavery Federalists waved aside complaints that the power could not be exercised until 1808. There was "more reason to rejoice that the power should be given at all, than to regret that its exercise should be postponed for twenty years."[19]

As its antislavery defenders saw it, the slave trade clause of the Constitution was calculated to encourage more states to abolish slavery on their own. In the words of one Federalist, "[t]he constitution says, by implication, to such states, —'well done ye good and faithful servants, continue your endeavors to compleat the glorious work.' "[20] This became the goal of all antislavery politics through the Civil War: Use federal power not only to prevent new slave states from forming in the territories but also to encourage existing slave states to abolish slavery on their own.

The antislavery commitment to state-by-state abolition was driven by an all-important constitutional principle that was not actually in the Constitution: the federal consensus. This was the assumption, nowhere explicitly stated in the document, that the federal government had no power to "interfere" with slavery, or abolition, in the states.[21] Like other "domestic institutions" such as marriage, apprenticeship, or indentured servitude, slavery remained the exclusive province of the states. "I apprehend that it is not in our power to do anything for, or against, those who are in slavery in the southern States," explained an antislavery delegate to the Massachusetts ratifying convention. No one "detests every idea of slavery more than I do," he went on, and he hoped the southern states would eventually follow the example of Massachusetts, but "we have no right to compel them."[22]

For seventy years, in every congressional debate over slavery, antislavery northerners went out of their way to acknowledge that Congress had no power to abolish slavery in a state.[23] In 1833 the radical abolitionists who formed the American Anti-Slavery Society recognized "the sovereignty of each state, to legislate exclusively on the subject of slavery which is tolerated within its limits."[24] In the 1840s both the Liberty Party and the Free Soil Party paid their respects to the federal consensus. In the 1850s even the most radical Republicans—Thaddeus Stevens, Charles Sumner, John Hale, Benjamin Wade—repeatedly affirmed the federal consensus, as did Abraham Lincoln. "I have no purpose, directly or indirectly, to interfere with the institution of slavery in the States where it exists," Lincoln said. "I believe I have no lawful right to do so, and I have no inclination to do so."[25] No actual clause in the Constitution restricted the scope of antislavery politics as much as this one principle that was not even in the Constitution.

Yet if the federal consensus shielded slavery in the states, it was also seen as a grant of power to the states to abolish slavery as well as a constitutional shelter that protected emancipation in the states where slavery was abolished. State abolition, one antislavery Federalist explained, "can *in no wise* be controuled or restrained by the federal legislature."[26] In 1790 a House committee dominated by antislavery members acknowledged that "Congress have no authority to interfere" with slavery in the states, though it was "equally restrained from interfering with the emancipation of slaves" in the states where slavery was being abolished.[27] Rufus King, a prominent Federalist, agreed. The Constitution "grants no power to congress to interfere" with slavery in a state, he declared in 1820; "the slave states therefore, are free to continue *or to abolish slavery.*"[28] In 1842 Ohio congressman Joshua Giddings invoked the Tenth Amendment to argue that the power to either abolish or legalize slavery was not delegated to the federal government and was therefore strictly reserved to the states.[29] The Constitution, he would admit, "regards slavery as strictly a State institution, over which the general government has no control whatsoever." But "the free States have rights as well as the slave States," Giddings added, "our right to be exempt from slavery, and from its expense, its guilt, and its disgrace, is supreme and unrestricted."[30] Among antislavery constitutionalists the logical conclusion of the federal consensus was the demand (issued by both the Liberty and Free Soil parties) that the federal government completely "divorce" itself from slavery.

Thus the federal consensus reflected the contradictory implications of a Constitution that was read as both proslavery and antislavery. Slavery was the only domestic institution the Constitution protected, albeit indirectly, by means of the three-fifths and fugitive slave clauses, *and* the only institution the federal government was empowered to move against, also indirectly, by banning slavery from the territories and shutting down the Atlantic slave trade. The federal consensus had similarly ambiguous implications. Proslavery southerners claimed—and antislavery northerners agreed—that the federal government could not constitutionally "interfere" with slavery in their states. But by the 1840s political abolitionists were drawing the additional inference that if the federal government could not interfere, neither could it protect slavery. Instead they called for "the absolute and unqualified divorce of the General Government from slavery."[31]

-»»«««-

IT HAS BEEN SAID that the meaning of the Constitution was not "fixed" in the convention at which the document was drafted nor in the debates over its ratification.[32] It is certainly the case that decades after ratification proslavery constitutionalists cited many different clauses of the Constitution that they believed justified federal protection of slavery. It is less well known that antislavery constitutionalists did the same thing, only in reverse. Over time they would colonize more and more of the Constitution and in the process steadily expand the scope of federal power to undermine slavery.

Antislavery constitutionalists freely acknowledged and openly deplored the proslavery elements in the Constitution. The three-fifths clause rankled the most because it tipped the balance of federal power in favor of the slave states by increasing the number of southerners in the House of Representatives and enhancing their power in the Electoral College. From the earliest years of the republic, antislavery critics denounced the three-fifths clause, and for decades to come they viewed it as the most egregious of the compromises made between pro-slavery and antislavery delegates at the Constitutional Convention. Yet despite its ambiguity, Article IV, Section 2—the fugitive slave clause—also had undeniable proslavery implications. It granted slaveholders a constitutional right to enforce southern slave laws in northern states where slavery had been abolished. These were the two great and lamentable exceptions, antislavery constitutionalists argued, in a Constitution that otherwise made freedom the rule.

There was not much to be done about the three-fifths clause short of a constitutional amendment repealing it, but the fugitive slave clause was different because it was intrinsically contradictory. It allowed the states to require due process in fugitive slave renditions *and* it allowed masters to recapture their slaves without due process. Over the years antislavery constitutionalists came to insist on a strict construction of the fugitive slave clause. They would whittle down its meaning, limit its reach, and undermine its effectiveness. They pointed out that it applied only to slaves escaping into free states. It did not apply to slaves who escaped into the territories, or foreign countries, or to slaves who rebelled on the high seas. Nor did it apply to slaves who were brought voluntarily into free states by their owners.

This reasoning opened the door to a series of northern statutes emancipating any slaves whose masters traveled with them into a free state.[33] These "sojourn" laws, as they are known, were based on the assumption that the Constitution guaranteed masters a right of recaption for *fugitive* slaves only, whereas northern state laws—like the Constitution itself—

presumed that anyone setting foot on free soil was free. A number of slaves (it's impossible to say how many) were thereby freed when their owners traveled with them into free states.

More importantly, antislavery constitutionalists insisted that the fugitive slave clause could not be enforced in disregard of the Fifth Amendment guarantee of due process. For this reason many of them viewed the two major fugitive slave laws passed by Congress in 1793 and 1850 as unconstitutional. In the decade before the Civil War some Republicans advocated open violations of the Fugitive Slave Act while others, notably Abraham Lincoln, called for obedience to the law so long as it remained on the books.[34] Virtually all antislavery politicians, including Lincoln, called for the repeal or revision of the 1850 law.

Far from denying that the founders had compromised with slavery in certain ways, antislavery constitutionalists highlighted those compromises whenever critics complained about northern interference with an institution that was strictly the business of the South. Lincoln was hardly alone in fingering the three-fifths clause as a humiliating discrimination against the free states, one that gave them a direct interest in preventing the admission of new slave states. So also did the Constitution compel free states to allow slaveholders to come within their borders and enforce laws that most northerners found offensive. Similarly, under the fifteenth clause of Article I, Section 8, the federal government could call up northern militias to suppress slave insurrections in the South. Critics of slavery routinely claimed that these passages of the Constitution made the future of slavery in the United States a national issue rather than a strictly sectional one. Accordingly, those same critics highlighted the Constitution's antislavery elements and consistently urged Congress to act on them.

Barely had the Constitution been ratified when opponents of slavery began petitioning Congress to undermine the institution to "the full extent" of its powers. Representatives should go "as far as they constitutionally could" to act against slavery "in all cases to which the authority of Congress extends."[35] These earliest calls for federal action were prompted by Quaker and abolitionist petitions in 1790 urging Congress to exercise all its power to inhibit the importation of slaves, well before the complete ban became available in 1808. Congress, the petitioners noted, could ban slave imports into the territories, tax every slave imported into the states, and prohibit foreign captains from plying their nefarious trade in American ports. Over the ensuing decades antislavery constitutionalists would repeatedly specify what the "full extent" of Congress's power was, pointing to various clauses of the Constitution that sanctioned congressional action against slavery and, not incidentally, provoking a proslavery response.

That conflict began in 1790 and never really ended until slavery was finally destroyed in 1865. At every step in between, as each new controversy arose, a proslavery Constitution developed, dialectically as it were, alongside its antislavery counterpart. The antislavery Constitution, then, was not the inexorable unfolding of the libertarian premises of the founding generation: it was the product of a series of often bitter political conflicts, some famous and others barely known. With each new debate the scope of proslavery and antislavery constitutionalism expanded. This became abundantly clear during the Missouri Crisis of 1820–21. By then each side's weapons were already sharpened by thirty years of political combat.

2

"Freedom Is the Rule, Slavery Is the Exception"

The Emergence of Antislavery Constitutionalism

I love the Constitution. It is enshrined in my heart. . . . All I want is to get the country back to the position, to the administrative policy, of the fathers. I want the Constitution that my fathers gave me, baptized in blood, and not the Constitution of Judge Taney.[1]

Owen Lovejoy, 1860

I n May of 1854 the US Congress, led by Illinois senator Stephen A. Douglas, repealed the ban on slavery in the Louisiana Purchase territories north of 36° 30′. The ban, excluding Missouri itself, had been put in place as part of the Missouri Compromise of 1820.

The repeal took Lincoln and his fellow northern Whigs by surprise. It "astounded us," he said. "We were thunderstruck and stunned."[2] Lincoln later recalled that in 1854 his law practice "had almost superseded the thought of politics," but that "the repeal of the Missouri compromise aroused him as he had never been before."[3] Though he had never been fully absent from Illinois politics, Lincoln nevertheless reemerged as the state's leading exponent of antislavery constitutionalism.

There's more than a little irony here. Back in 1820, when Missouri applied for admission to the Union as a slave state, antislavery northerners overwhelmingly rejected the so-called compromise. They viewed it as a victory for the proslavery forces in Congress. Thirty-four years later, antislavery northerners were "thunderstruck" when that same compromise was repealed, a repeal they denounced as yet another proslavery victory. The connecting link—the consistency, if you will—between 1820 and 1854 lies in the constitutional doctrine of slavery's opponents. For it was during the Missouri Crisis that northern representatives in Congress brought together the various strands of antislavery constitutional thought into a coherent critique of slavery. Three decades later, in his first major antislavery speech, Abraham Lincoln based his own denunciation of the repeal of the Missouri Compromise on a fully evolved antislavery constitutionalism.

In 1820 an antislavery voting bloc encompassed a majority of northerners in the House of Representatives. Over the course of the next decade that northern majority provoked a number of debates over slavery and in the process added new dimensions to the earlier antislavery interpretations of the Constitution. Representatives from the free states asserted a constitutional right to require a territory to abolish slavery as a condition for admission to the Union. Similarly, opponents of slavery claimed that Congress could, under the Constitution, abolish slavery in Washington, DC. In 1821 northern congressmen objected when Missouri applied for admission to the Union with a constitution that denied free Blacks the privileges and immunities to which they were entitled as citizens of northern states. Later in the decade, a fierce debate over the Negro Seaman Act passed by South Carolina led northerners to insist that free Black sailors entering southern ports were entitled to the due process rights guaranteed by the Fifth Amendment. Each of the constitutional principles enunciated in these debates became permanent fixtures of antislavery constitutionalism, with momentous consequences for the nationwide debate over slavery.

-»)«&-

IN 1820 Congressman James Tallmadge Jr. of New York introduced two antislavery amendments to the Missouri statehood bill. The first would ban all future importations of slaves into the state. The second would require Missouri to implement an abolition program similar to those adopted in the northeastern states. Tallmadge based his amendments on Article IV, Section 3, of the Constitution, which declares that "new States may be admitted by Congress into this Union." To ensure that no more slave states applied for admission to the Union, Tallmadge urged that a ban on slavery in the territories "be extended from the Mississippi river to the Pacific ocean." The Constitution, Tallmadge noted, authorized Congress "to make all needful Rules and Regulations respecting the Territory." Congress regularly imposed a number of conditions in statehood bills, so why not abolition?[4] Moreover, slavery was incompatible with republicanism, and does not Section 4—the so-called guarantee clause—specifically require the US government to "guarantee to every State in this Union a Republican Form of Government"?[5] Although this reading of Article IV went beyond banning slavery in all US territories, it was widely popular among northerners.

Free-state representatives supported Tallmadge's first amendment by a vote of 84–10 and his second amendment, requiring abolition as a condition for statehood, by a vote of 80–14. By 1820, then, the overwhelming majority of northern congressmen assumed that the Constitution's territorial and guarantee clauses vested the federal government with considerable antislavery powers. Not only could Congress ban the admission of slaves into any US territory, it could require that territory to abolish slavery as a condition for admission to the Union.

Several features of the proslavery Constitution also made their impressive debut in the Missouri debates and the immediately preceding debate over the admission of Arkansas. Until then it was taken for granted that Congress could ban slavery from the territories, a power the slaveholders themselves had acknowledged. But in 1819, for the first time, slaveholders in Congress began to deny that the federal government had the power to impose such a ban. They based this claim on the argument that the fugitive slave clause of the Constitution guaranteed a general right of "property in man."

This unprecedented proslavery position developed in response to the strikingly aggressive antislavery congressmen who not only provoked the crisis but refused to back down. When slaveholders complained that restricting slavery from the territories violated their property rights, antislavery constitutionalists replied that the Constitution did not recognize slaves as "property," only as "persons," and that the federal government was under no obligation to enforce rights unique to individual states.

Antislavery northerners went still further, claiming that the federal government was under no obligation to protect rights created by individual states—such as the right of property in man. Rufus King distinguished "federal rights," which were "uniform throughout the union," from "rights derived from the constitution and laws of the states" and as such were enforceable only in those states. The "error," John Taylor argued, "is in confounding the rights of United States citizenship with those arising under the laws of Kentucky." The right to hold slaves as property, Taylor insisted, "is not derived from the Federal Constitution."[6] Whereas state-derived rights were unenforceable beyond the limits of the states that created them, federal rights applied everywhere. The privileges and immunities of citizens were general, antislavery northerners claimed—they were enjoyed by all citizens in every state. In particular they applied to Blacks who were citizens of northern states and as such were constitutionally entitled to move freely from one state to another. This was the issue at stake in the second Missouri crisis of 1821.

After having secured the right to enter the Union as a slave state despite the opposition of a majority of northern congressmen, Missouri came back the following year with a proposed constitution that authorized the state legislature "to pass such laws as may be necessary . . . to prevent free negroes and mulattoes from coming to, and settling in this state, under any pretext whatsoever." Once again a majority of northern congressmen objected, this time on the ground that Missouri's proposal violated the privileges and immunities clause of the Constitution. Rhode Island senator James Burrill denounced the Missouri proposal as "entirely repugnant to the Constitution." Blacks were recognized as citizens in Massachusetts, for example. Was it possible for Missouri, "consistently with the Constitution, to exclude any of those citizens of Massachusetts from the State?" If Missouri's constitution "excluded altogether" any free man "who is a citizen of another State of this Union," Pennsylvania congressman John Sergeant declared, "then it is impossible to reconcile that constitution with the Constitution of the United States."[7] Even as they defended the privileges and immunities of Black northerners, antislavery spokesmen denied that the federal government was obliged to recognize or protect a right of "property in man," on the grounds that it was a state rather than a US constitutional right.

The Missouri Crisis established the templates for all subsequent congressional debates between proslavery and antislavery constitutionalists. Unlike the ratification debates of the 1780s, opponents of slavery did not pick out one or two clauses of the Constitution for denunciation or defense. In 1820 northerners cited various clauses to justify a more general claim that the Constitution itself was an antislavery document. This was antislavery constitutionalism, fully articulated though not yet fully formed.

On May 13, 1826, Congressman Charles Miner called for "a bill for the gradual abolition of slavery in the District of Columbia, and such restrictions upon the Slave Trade therein as shall be just and proper."[8] No vote was taken and Miner's resolution simply died. Four years later, on January 6, 1829, Miner once again proposed that the Committee on the District of Columbia "inquire into the expediency of providing by law for the gradual abolition of slavery within the District." This time Miner did not specify how gradual abolition would take place, only that "the interests of no individual shall be injured thereby."[9] In the preamble to his resolution Miner was careful to cite the clause of the Constitution granting Congress the power to "exercise exclusive legislation" over the District. Defending the resolution, he emphasized that he had "set forth the constitutional power of Congress over this District."[10] Lincoln endorsed this view a decade later, and it remained a standard precept of anti-slavery politics that the "exclusive legislation" clause of the Constitution empowered Congress to abolish slavery in the District of Columbia.

Beyond the halls of Congress another dispute between slave and free states erupted in 1822 when South Carolina passed a law requiring the arrest and detention of any Black seamen serving on northern ships docked in Charleston. The first to protest the practice were the ship captains who filed a writ of habeas corpus demanding the release of the Black seamen on the grounds that they were "native citizens of the United States" who had been jailed "without a writ or any crime alleged."[11] Northern Blacks condemned the Negro Seaman Act as "manifestly unconstitutional; insomuch as the Constitution declares that the citizens of each State shall be entitled to all the rights and immunities of citizens of the several States."[12] Abolitionists took up the cause in the 1830s, and the conflict between northern and southern states would persist into the 1840s. But from the moment the ship captains petitioned Congress to protect the constitutional rights of Black sailors jailed in southern ports, due process and habeas corpus became fixtures of antislavery constitutionalism. In the early 1830s Black activists began calling for jury trials for accused fugitives, as did the American Anti-Slavery Society in 1833.

In defending the citizenship rights of African Americans, northern opponents of slavery opened a two-front war, the one between the slave and free states over slavery, the other over racial discrimination within the free states. While antislavery congressmen objected to Missouri's proposal to ban the immigration of free Blacks, other northern states were doing just that. The first generation of abolitionists in the late eighteenth century assumed that emancipation was the first step toward full citizenship for freed people.[13] In many northern states, and even in North Carolina, Black men voted on the same terms as white men. But racial discrimination waxed as antislavery politics waned. After 1800, but especially in the 1820s, a reaction set in and northern states began to strip Black men of the vote and pass laws banning the migration of African Americans into their states. It became clear that more northerners objected to slavery than to racial discrimination. Those overwhelming congressional votes to abolish slavery in Missouri did not automatically translate into state legislative votes in favor of Black civil and political rights. But laws discriminating against free Blacks often prompted divisive fights in those same northern legislatures where opponents of slavery were most likely to support some degree of racial equality.

By 1830 the antislavery Constitution encompassed far more than the slave trade clause that antislavery northerners had focused on during the ratification debates. Opponents of slavery were already claiming the territorial clause, the guarantee clause, the exclusive legislation clause, the privileges and immunities clause, and the Fifth Amendment in their efforts to restrict and undermine slavery. They defended Congress's power to ban slavery from all the territories, to require a state to abolish slavery as a condition for admission to the Union, and to abolish slavery in the District of Columbia. Many antislavery politicians, committed to the principle of fundamental human equality, attacked various forms of racial discrimination. They claimed that free Blacks were citizens of the United States by birthright and that with citizenship came a number of constitutionally protected privileges and immunities. No state could constitutionally prevent a citizen, Black or white, from migrating freely to another state. Nor could any state arbitrarily jail northern Black sailors and deprive them of their due process rights.

Throughout the 1820s these positions were openly proclaimed by mainstream politicians.

That changed in the 1830s, as national political parties successfully shut down most antislavery politics. The lesson party leaders took from the Missouri Crisis was that the politics of slavery were so disruptive that they could sunder the Union if not kept under control. Under what scholars call the Second Party System, the two major parties—the Demo-

crats and the Whigs—both had strong northern and southern wings. Both therefore actively avoided sectional divisions
within their ranks by suppressing the issue of slavery. Filling
the void was a newly militant abolitionist movement that took
up the banner of antislavery constitutionalism and further
expanded its boundaries.

The founding of the American Anti-Slavery Society in
1833 initiated more than two decades of extraordinary intellectual creativity among antislavery constitutionalists. For
example, in 1836 Samuel Prentiss invoked the constitutional
right of petition in defense of those who were demanding
the abolition of slavery in Washington, DC.[14] In 1837 Salmon
P. Chase pointed out that the fugitive slave clause recognized
fugitives as servants—"persons held to service"—and as such
entitled them to the constitutional protections afforded to all
such "persons."[15] In 1838, the abolitionist Theodore Dwight
Weld argued that the Constitution's Preamble authorized
the federal government to "establish justice" and "promote
the general welfare," making it a "grant of power" to Congress to abolish slavery in Washington, DC.[16] In 1839 the abolitionist William Jay invoked the Tenth Amendment to deny
that the federal government had any authority to protect
slavery in ways not specifically delegated to it. At the same
time he introduced the forfeiture-of-rights doctrine, warning that the few constitutional protections slaveholders did
have would be forfeited by any state that seceded from the
Union. They would, for example, forfeit their right to recapture fugitive slaves.[17]

Jay's insight concluded a decade in which antislavery radicals, led by African American activists, began arguing that

due process rights for alleged fugitives went beyond habeas corpus to include the right to jury trials. The "decision *of a jury* should be required," James Forten suggested in 1832, "upon so high a question as the liberty of a man."[18] Free Blacks had a compelling motive to demand such protections, for even in the North they could be kidnapped and sent into slavery without any right to defend their freedom in the courts. But the issue went beyond the self-defense of free Blacks. In the northern states where freedom was presumed, *all* those accused of being fugitive slaves were entitled to a proper legal defense and a jury trial. In 1835, Black New Yorkers who had organized a "Committee of Vigilance" resolved that accused fugitives were entitled to due process. As "the trial by jury is the great bulwark of the liberties of freemen," the committee declared, "it is RIGHT that the privileges of the same be extended to all persons claimed as fugitive slaves."[19] In 1837, led by David Ruggles, Black civil rights activists in New York called on the state legislature to "grant a *trial by jury* for their liberty to persons of color within this State arrested and claimed as fugitive slaves."[20] Others denounced the 1793 Fugitive Slave Act for denying due process rights to accused fugitives. In 1838 a mass meeting of Blacks in Philadelphia issued a lengthy "Appeal" which, among many other things, cited the Fifth Amendment guarantee that no person could be deprived of liberty without due process of law, "by which is certainly meant a TRIAL BY JURY."[21]

White abolitionists joined the chorus. "It is plain," the American Anti-Slavery Society declared in 1833, that those demanding the return of an alleged fugitive "are compelled to substantiate their claims before a *jury* by due process of law."[22] Soon antislavery politicians in the northern states were insisting that fugitive slaves were entitled to both habeas corpus and jury trials. Accused fugitives were likewise covered by the Fourth Amendment protection against unreasonable seizure. By 1850 the nation was thrown into crisis when masses of northerners, Black and white, protested a new fugitive slave law by which the federal government for the first time explicitly deprived accused fugitives of due process. Lincoln himself would insist on due process rights for alleged fugitives in his first inaugural address.

The war powers clause was also invoked for its antislavery implications beginning in the 1830s. The pioneering voice here was former president and now congressman John Quincy Adams. Opponents of slavery frequently complained that the Constitution compelled the free states to help suppress slave insurrections in the South, but Adams gave that proslavery reading an antislavery spin. Should the federal government be called on to suppress an insurrection or repel an invasion of the South, Adams argued, the war powers clause of the Constitution empowered the federal government to emancipate slaves in the process. The United States had long recognized the right of belligerents to liberate slaves in wartime, and in that sense the emancipatory power was already implied in the Constitution.[23] But Adams made the implicit explicit, arguing that the conditions of war and insurrection rendered the federal consensus irrelevant. Should federal authorities be called on to suppress a rebellion in a slave state, Congress could, in that case, "interfere" with slavery by freeing the slaves of rebellious masters.[24]

➤➤❭❬❬❬

As ABOLITIONISTS and antislavery politicians were colonizing more and more of the Constitution, antislavery constitutional thought was widening in a different way. Throughout
the 1830s William Lloyd Garrison endorsed the basic principles of antislavery constitutionalism, but by 1845 he had
dramatically shifted ground and was denouncing the Constitution as a "covenant with death" and "an agreement with
hell."[25] In those same years another group of radicals—
William Goodell, Alvan Stewart, Lysander Spooner, and
others—pushed in the opposite direction by arguing that
the Constitution was an abolitionist document.[26] Where the
Garrisonians abandoned their original position and now
claimed that the Constitution was so proslavery that the only
course of action for abolitionists was for the free states to
secede from the Union, Goodell and his followers held that
the federal government was fully empowered to abolish slavery everywhere.

As early as 1842 Garrison's paper, *The Liberator,* urged the
separation of the free and slave states on the grounds that
"slavery is the supreme law of the land, and an integral part
of the national compact."[27] In 1844 Garrison's intellectually
formidable ally, Wendell Phillips, published *The Constitution
a Proslavery Compact,* the first full-scale denunciation of the
Constitution by an antislavery radical. Where most antislavery activists pointed to the numerous clauses of the Constitution that favored freedom over slavery, Phillips narrowed
his focus to the few passages that referred directly to slavery, most notably the three-fifths and fugitive slave clauses.

Though he acknowledged that those clauses were ambiguous, he pointed out that the proslavery reading was the one that prevailed among all the branches of the federal government. At "this time and for the last half century," Phillips argued, "the Constitution of the United States, has been, and still is, a pro-slavery instrument."[28] He thereby created the model later adopted by historians who viewed the Constitution as a proslavery document.

William Goodell, arguing for an abolitionist Constitution, carefully separated two issues that Phillips had joined together. The first was what the Constitution actually said about slavery and freedom. The second was how the Slave Power—the proslavery politicians who dominated the federal government—succeeded in imposing their own proslavery interpretation of the Constitution in national policy.[29] The question of whether the Constitution supported slavery or freedom must be answered "*not* in respect to any, or to all the successive *administrations* of the National Government," Goodell argued, "but in regard to its original organic structure—its inherent nature and character—*its Constitutional Law.*" It was a commonplace among slavery's critics that the federal government had long pursued policies favorable to slavery, but they believed those policies violated both the letter and the spirit of the Constitution. Is the Constitution of the United States "what it professes, in its Preamble, to be?" Goodell asked. If the national government was in fact established to "secure *liberty,*" the only question is whether "it is *competent to do the things* promised to the People, and to their posterity, in its Preamble." Most antislavery constitutionalists argued that freedom was national and slavery merely local.

Goodell disputed this. To say that the federal government "can secure *general liberty*, and at the same time guarantee *local slavery*," he declared, "is to affirm the greatest of moral absurdities" and "deny self-evident truths."[30] If the Constitution was what its Preamble proclaimed it to be, Goodell concluded, the federal government had all the power it needed to abolish slavery in every locality.

African American activists often felt a special loyalty to Garrison for his untiring advocacy of the civic equality of Blacks, but they disagreed among themselves about his denunciation of the Constitution. To be sure, Garrison had his supporters. The "Constitution of the United States is proslavery," H. Ford Douglas declared. It was "considered so by those who framed it, and construed to that end ever since its adoption." But William Howard Day disputed Douglas's reading of the Constitution. "If it says it was framed to 'establish justice,' it, of course, is opposed to injustice; if it says plainly that no person shall be deprived of 'life, *liberty*, of property, without due process of law,'—I suppose it means it, and I shall avail myself of the benefit of it."[31] At a State Convention of the Colored Citizens of Ohio in 1851, John Mercer Langston denounced the Fugitive Slave Act of 1850 on the familiar grounds of antislavery constitutionalism. The offending statute "kills alike, the true spirit of the American Declaration of Independence, the Constitution, and the palladium of our liberties." Frederick Douglass publicly renounced his earlier support for the Garrisonian interpretation and by 1860 was among the most effective spokesmen for Goodell's view of the Constitution as an abolitionist document.

Despite this widened spectrum of abolitionist thought

about the Constitution, most opponents of slavery avoided the two poles.[32] They rejected Garrisonian disunion outright and insisted that, on the contrary, the founders had created an antislavery Union. They believed, unlike Goodell, that the federal government could not abolish slavery in a state, but that the federal government was authorized to implement a number of antislavery policies that would lead to slavery's ultimate extinction.

➤➤❮❮❮

IN THE LATE 1840S antislavery politicians brought the various elements of antislavery constitutional thought together in a powerful synthesis centered on the rights of due process, especially habeas corpus.[33] The antislavery synthesis developed over the course of the decade, beginning with a debate over the status of slavery on the high seas and in foreign ports. In 1840 John C. Calhoun proposed a series of Senate resolutions declaring that the property rights of southern slaveholders followed the American flag on ships around the world, even in British ports where slavery had been abolished. Michigan senator Augustus S. Porter rejected Calhoun's view and argued instead that in British territory habeas corpus "reaches" the slave and "must liberate him." Porter's reasoning was familiar: In British ports slave owners could not point to a statute that allowed them to hold anyone in slavery against his or her will.[34]

An antislavery principle that originated in a dispute over the status of slaves in British ports soon expanded into a claim about slaves anywhere on the high seas. In 1842, as if in reply to Calhoun's proslavery Senate resolutions of two years earlier, Joshua Giddings proposed a number of antislavery resolutions to the House of Representatives. Once slaves were carried beyond the borders of a state and onto the high seas, "the persons on board cease to be subject to the slave laws of such State," Giddings reasoned, and are thereafter governed by the laws of the United States. Slaves who rebel onboard were merely "resuming their natural rights of personal liberty," Giddings argued, and were violating no US laws. Any attempt to re-enslave the rebels was "unauthorized by the Constitution or the laws of the United States."[35] For Calhoun, slavery followed the flag onto the high seas and around the world; for Giddings, the laws of slavery lost all their force once a ship left the port of a slave state. For his insistent radicalism Giddings was censured by his colleagues and resigned from the House. Yet he was doubly vindicated. He was quickly reelected to Congress by the overwhelming majority of his constituents. And by the end of the decade his radical claim—that beyond the borders of the southern states slaves were protected by the Constitution—entered the mainstream of antislavery politics as the focus shifted from slavery on the high seas to slavery in the territories.

The annexation of Texas in December 1845 and the ensuing war against Mexico pushed the issue of slavery's expansion into the center of American politics. A majority of northern congressmen supported a proviso introduced by Pennsylvania congressman David Wilmot that would ban slavery from all the territory taken from Mexico—a vast expanse that included what are now the states of California, Nevada,

Arizona, New Mexico, and Utah. Calhoun countered the Wilmot Proviso by expanding on the principle he had enunciated back in 1840. Slavery, he argued, followed the Constitution into the territories just as it followed the flag onto the high seas and into foreign ports. Attempting to resolve the impasse between proslavery and antislavery forces, Delaware senator John M. Clayton proposed a compromise that would allow the issue to be settled by the Supreme Court. Skeptics wondered how a territorial case could come to the Supreme Court, and the answer was that a slave carried into a territory could sue on a writ of habeas corpus.[36] Clayton's compromise failed, but for antislavery constitutionalists an important principle had been introduced.

In 1848 Gamaliel Bailey spelled out that principle in an influential editorial in his abolitionist newspaper, *The National Era*. Bailey began from the premise that the bulk of the Constitution favored freedom and that slavery should be "treated as an exception, entitled only to exceptional safeguards, by the Constitution of the United States." The Fourth Amendment expressly prohibits unreasonable searches and seizures, Bailey noted, and the Fifth Amendment prohibits Congress from depriving anyone of their liberty without due process of law. Under the Tenth Amendment, Congress "can exercise no power not conferred upon it in express terms by the Federal Constitution." If every "person" in the territories was protected by the sovereign authority of the Constitution, it followed that Congress could not constitutionally *allow* slavery into the territories. Or as Bailey put it, "the Constitution positively prohibits the General Government from creating slavery."[37] As territorial governments were creatures of Congress, they too were forbidden by the Constitution to legalize slavery.

The Free Soil platform of 1848 reflected this radical new theory by fusing the Preamble of the Constitution to the Fifth Amendment. The founders had created a national government whose purpose was to "secure the blessings of Liberty," Free Soilers declared, "but expressly *denied* to the Federal Government, which they created, all constitutional power to *deprive any person* of life, *liberty*, or property, without due legal process." It followed that "Congress has no more power to make a SLAVE than to make a KING."[38]

With that deceptively simple insight, the debate over slavery permanently shifted. Freedom, not slavery, followed the Constitution, and any slaves carried into US territory could sue for their liberty under a writ of habeas corpus. It was no longer enough to say that Congress should ban slavery from the territories. If freedom followed the Constitution, Congress had no authority to *allow* slavery into the territories.

The same constitutional issues arose, also in the late 1840s, in the increasingly contentious debate over fugitive slaves. Clearly the Constitution gave slavery "extraterritorial" claims in the free states. But what claims? Antislavery constitutionalists argued that alleged fugitive slaves captured in a free state were entitled to the presumption of freedom and the due process rights that all persons were entitled to. They could sue their captors under a writ of habeas corpus and demand a jury trial in which slaveholders would be compelled to prove their claims of ownership.[39] As New York senator William Seward put it, the Fugitive Slave Act of

1793 was unconstitutional because it "deprives the alleged refugee . . . of the writ of *habeas corpus*, and of any certain judicial process."[40] Yes, there is a fugitive slave clause in the Constitution, antislavery politicians noted, but there's also a Fifth Amendment. Even if the fugitive slave clause implied a federal grant of power to enforce fugitive slave renditions, Salmon P. Chase argued, Congress was "bound" to exercise it "with careful regard, not merely to the alleged right sought to be secured, but to every other right which may be affected by it."[41] The fugitive slave clause recognized an owner's right to recover a fugitive slave, but it could not be enforced in disregard of the constitutional right to due process.

African Americans remained particularly vocal in the debate. The new Fugitive Slave Act of 1850 provoked an unprecedented wave of militancy among northern Blacks precisely because it explicitly stripped accused fugitives of the rights of due process. In 1859 John Mercer Langston defended the dramatic rescue of John Price, a fugitive slave at Oberlin, Ohio, by a crowd of Blacks and whites. The rescuers were said to have vindicated the proposition that "the humblest human being" was entitled to Fifth Amendment protections. Langston's brother, Charles H. Langston, defended his participation in the rescue in a moving speech in which he proclaimed that "the Constitution of the U.S. guarantees, not merely to its citizens, but *to all persons*, a trial before an *impartial* jury."[42] A year earlier a convention of Ohio Blacks had declared their veneration of the Declaration of Independence and the Constitution of the United States, as well as their readiness "to support and defend that system of government which finds its foundation in these great documents of freedom." Nevertheless, the delegates resolved, "we trample the Fugitive Slave Act and the dicta of the Dred Scott decision beneath our feet, as huge outrages, not only upon the Declaration of Independence and the Constitution of the United States, but upon humanity itself."[43]

By the 1850s antislavery politicians commonly based the rights of accused fugitives on Article IV, Section 2, of the Constitution, the privileges and immunities clause. As far back as 1821 a majority of northerners in Congress had been prepared to defend the privileges and immunities of free Blacks, whom they considered citizens of their states. In the 1830s and 1840s northern states had passed a series of "personal liberty" laws based on the assumption that free African Americans, born and raised in the United States, were citizens by birthright and as such were entitled to the "privileges and immunities" of citizenship. The Constitution itself was silent as to what those privileges and immunities were, and there was as yet no federal civil rights law or Fourteenth Amendment to specify them.[44] But Blacks and whites who were struggling against both slavery in the South and racial discrimination in the North insisted that all citizens had the right to buy and sell property, to sue, to move freely from one state to another, and to make and enforce contracts. They also had the right to trial by jury and habeas corpus.

Early on, birthright citizenship became a staple of Black political thought.[45] In 1849, citing Article II, Section 1, and Article IV, Section 2, a Convention of the Colored Citizens of Ohio declared that "the Constitution of our common country gives us citizenship." We are "coming for our rights," they added, "coming through the Constitution of our common country."[46] These were rights useful in the struggle against racial discrimination as well as slavery. In 1842 Charles Lenox Remond denounced segregated trains and streetcars as a violation of "the rights, privileges and immunities" of citizenship.[47] In 1853 William Nell organized a petition drive to lift the ban on Blacks in the Massachusetts militia—a ban, the petitioners asserted, that was "at war with the American Constitution."[48] Three years later a convention of Ohio Blacks demanded the right to vote on the basis of "a proper appreciation of the Declaration of Independence and our Bill of Rights."[49] For African Americans the Constitution was more than an antislavery document. It also recognized their citizenship as a birthright, one that entitled them to all of citizenship's privileges.[50]

African Americans had important white allies in the entwined struggles against slavery in the South and racial discrimination in the North. In 1838 William Yates specified a number of legal rights he attributed to citizenship in a pioneering essay on "The Rights of Colored Men."[51] Four years later Joshua Giddings issued a radical assault on the Fugitive Slave Act of 1793 in which he argued that "as a citizen of our State" a free African American in Ohio "may defend himself against a person who, without process, attempts to arrest him for a crime."[52] By the 1850s even relatively conservative opponents of slavery, men like Roger Baldwin, denounced the new Fugitive Slave Act on the grounds that it denied due process rights to free Blacks who were "as much entitled to the rights of citizens as are men of any other color or complexion whatsoever."[53] At the other end of the antislavery spectrum, Charles Sumner complained that the 1850 Fugitive Slave

Act denied accused fugitives of the due process rights that "belong to the safeguards of the citizen."[54] By then the privileges and immunities clause occupied an important place within mainstream antislavery constitutionalism, alongside the Preamble, the guarantee clause, the "needful rules and regulations" and exclusive legislation clauses, the war powers clause, and of course the Fourth, Fifth, and Tenth amendments.

->>)«<-

ANTISLAVERY CONSTITUTIONALISM did not rely solely on these various clauses in the text. Its advocates also invoked what they called the "spirit" of the Constitution—the spirit of universal liberty explicitly proclaimed in the Preamble but whose guiding inspiration was the Declaration of Independence. This was a well-established feature of the antislavery constitutional tradition. James Forten was hardly alone when in 1813 he discerned the principle of fundamental human equality embedded within "that glorious fabric of collected wisdom, our noble Constitution."[55] In 1820 John Taylor invited his fellow congressmen to name "the principles on which the United States Government is founded." Reciting the words of the Declaration of Independence, Taylor pointed out that "Congress, within its sovereignty, has constantly endeavored to prevent the extension of slavery, and has maintained the doctrine 'that all men are born equally free.'"[56] A convention of People of Colour in Philadelphia in 1831 resolved to read both the Declaration of Independence and the Constitution at all future meetings, "believing, that the truths contained in the former are incontrovertible, and that the latter guarantees in letter and spirit to every freeman born in this country, all the rights and immunities of citizenship."[57] Two years later the radical abolitionists who met in the same city to form the American Anti-Slavery Society declared that the "corner stone" of the republic was the universal right to freedom, and that "the highest obligations resting upon the people of the free states [was] to remove slavery by moral and political action, as prescribed in the Constitution of the United States." An 1840 "Convention of Colored Citizens" in Albany, New York, resolved that the Declaration of Independence and the Constitution "may be considered as more fully developing the primary ideas of American republicanism, than any other documents."[58] In 1844 the abolitionist Liberty Party proclaimed in its platform that "no other party in the country represents the true principles of American liberty, or the true spirit of the Constitution of the United States."

African American activists were adamant that the principle of fundamental human equality was the philosophical basis of the Constitution. The "fathers of the Revolution," a Detroit convention of "Colored Citizens" declared in 1840, announced "those noble principles set forth in the Declaration of Independence which declares that 'all men are born free and equal' . . . and thereupon established the Constitution of the United States."[59] In 1853 a Colored National Convention meeting in Rochester issued an address declaring that "ALL MEN ARE CREATED EQUAL" and that "THE CONSTITUTION OF THE UNITED STATES WAS FORMED TO ESTABLISH JUSTICE, PROMOTE THE

GENERAL WELFARE, AND SECURE THE BLESSING OF
LIBERTY TO ALL THE PEOPLE OF THIS COUNTRY."[60]

Similar fusions of the Declaration of Independence and
the Constitution appeared in the platforms of every antislavery political party in the 1840s and 1850s. In 1848 the
Free Soilers invoked the Declaration of Independence just
before paraphrasing the Preamble by declaring that "our
fathers ordained the Constitution" in order to "establish justice, promote the general welfare, [and] secure the blessings
of liberty." Eight years later, the new Republican Party did
the same thing. With "our Republican fathers," the party
resolved, "we hold it to be a self-evident truth, that all men
are endowed with the inalienable right to life, liberty, and
the pursuit of happiness, and that the primary object and
ulterior design of our Federal Government were to secure
these rights to all persons under its exclusive jurisdiction." So
claimed the Republicans in 1856.

BY THEN the spirit and the text had combined to give antislavery constitutionalism a simple but powerful organizing
theme: "Freedom is the rule, slavery is the exception."[61] So
popular was this formulation among antislavery northerners, from the most conservative to the most radical, that
today we would refer to it as a sound bite. Horace Mann,
denying that the Constitution recognized slaves as property,
concluded: "Freedom is the rule, slavery is the exception."[62]
New York congressman Benjamin F. Butler endorsed the sentiment. "[W]herever the flag of our country is unfurled," he

declared, "Freedom is the general and cherished rule, Slavery the partial and much-lamented exception."[63] According to Lincoln's friend Edward D. Baker, "the entire population of the North and West are devoted, in the very depths of their hearts, to the great constitutional idea that freedom is the rule, that slavery is the exception."[64]

A substantial antislavery politics was possible under a Constitution that made freedom the rule and slavery the exception. Although the federal consensus prevented Congress from interfering with slavery *in* the states, it also restricted slavery *to* the states. This, as antislavery constitutionalists understood it, placed a number of restraints on slaveholders. The antislavery Constitution denied the slaveholders' claims of property outside their own states, denied them the right to carry their slaves into the territories, denied them a property claim on slaves who escaped to free states, and denied them any claim to slaves who rebelled on the high seas or ended up in the ports of nations where slavery was abolished.

Conversely, the Constitution empowered Congress to prevent states from importing slaves, to suppress the coastwise slave trade, thwart slavery's expansion, deny admission to new slave states, abolish slavery in Washington, DC, and protect the due process rights of accused fugitives. If the slave states seceded, the federal government could emancipate slaves in an effort to suppress the rebellion. Meanwhile the rebellious states would forfeit their limited right to recapture fugitives. By 1860 the mainstream of antislavery constitutionalism posited a Constitution that, from the Preamble to the Tenth Amendment, was peppered with a dozen or so clauses that privileged freedom, clauses that positively enjoined

Congress from protecting slavery while expressly requiring it to protect freedom and equality.

Slavery's defenders, outraged by the growing breadth and popularity of antislavery constitutionalism, fought back with an increasingly aggressive proslavery constitutionalism. Not only were slaves property, the Constitution "expressly" recognized them as such in the fugitive slave clause. The Fifth Amendment prevented the federal government from depriving masters of their property without due process of law. Because slaves were a constitutionally protected "species of property," Congress had no authority to abolish slavery in Washington, DC. The Constitution carried slavery onto the high seas and into the territories where it protected the master's right of "property in man." The same right of property followed the fugitive slave into the free states. By the 1850s proslavery constitutionalists abandoned their earlier claims that the federal government had no authority over slavery anywhere. Now, they argued, Congress was positively obliged to enforce the fugitive slave clause in the northern states, to protect the rights of slaveholders in foreign ports, and to impose a federal slave code on territories that refused to pass such codes on their own. Because the Constitution recognized slaves as property, the federal government would have to protect the property rights of slaveholders everywhere.

But if, as slavery's opponents believed, the Constitution recognized slaves not as property but as "persons," the federal government was obligated to protect the rights of all persons under its sovereign jurisdiction. The denial of the property right, long the foundational principle of the antislavery Constitution, was the openly proclaimed position of the Republican Party. Salmon P. Chase called property in man a "naked legal right" that existed only within the states that legalized slavery.[65] "I deny that the Constitution recognizes property in man," William Seward declared in 1850. The only thing the Constitution contains "are two incidental allusions to slaves," the three-fifths and the fugitive slave clauses. But these "incidental" references paled beside the Constitution's overwhelming antislavery thrust, Seward insisted. Slavery was "only *one* of many institutions" recognized by the Constitution; "freedom is equally an institution there." There was, however, a difference between the two institutions. "Slavery is only a temporary, accidental, partial and incongruous one," Seward argued; "freedom, on the contrary, is a perpetual, organic, universal one, in harmony with the Constitution of the United States."[66] This made the Constitution compatible with what Seward called the "higher law," for both were committed to the principle of universal freedom. Far from repudiating the Constitution as a pact with Satan, the vast majority of antislavery leaders embraced it. "We have the example of our fathers on our side," Chase declared. "We have the Constitution of their adoption on our side."[67]

⇢ 3 ⇠

The Antislavery Project

Lincoln and Antislavery Politics

ON FEBRUARY 22, 1856, Abraham Lincoln was the featured speaker at a convention of newspaper editors meeting in Decatur, Illinois, the immediate precursor to the first formal gathering of the Illinois Republican Party.[1] The convention had endorsed a set of resolutions that were copied almost verbatim from the resolutions of an earlier Anti-Nebraska convention held in Quincy.[2] The delegates resolved to abide by all the constitutional rights the slave states were entitled to and affirmed the federal consensus, disclaiming any "purpose to annoy or disturb our sister States in the peaceful enjoyment of any of their rights." But the editors also insisted that the right of property in slaves existed only "within the jurisdiction" of the slave states themselves. They called for the "restriction of Slavery to its present authorized limits" and implied that no new slave states should be admitted to the Union. Territories have no "constitutional right to demand admittance into the sisterhood of States" whereas

Congress had a "*duty*" to prevent "any poisonous matter" from entering "into our extremities." In addition to specific policies, the delegates endorsed the basic principle of antislavery constitutionalism:

> We hold that our general government is imbued throughout the whole organization with the spirit of Liberty, as set forth originally in the Declaration of Independence . . . ; that it recognized FREEDOM as the *rule* and SLAVERY as the *exception* . . . , and that it nowhere sanctions the idea of *property in man* as one of its principles.[3]

That evening, the convention's work done, Lincoln spoke for half an hour "in his usual masterly manner, frequently interrupted by the cheers of his hearers."[4]

Most of what Lincoln had to say about slavery and the Constitution was packed into the six years between the Peoria address in late 1854 and his first inaugural address in early 1861. But in those years Lincoln proved an eloquent, if unoriginal, advocate for the antislavery constitutional tradition. He repeatedly insisted that the Constitution recognized slaves only as persons, never as property. He vowed to abide by the federal consensus by not interfering directly with slavery in the states where it existed, but he denounced the tendency to spread proslavery constitutional principles into the free states. He always said that the guiding spirit of the Constitution was the principle of fundamental human equality proclaimed in the Declaration of Independence. The antislavery Constitution shaped his antislavery politics. Lincoln believed that Congress could, "under the Constitution," abolish slavery in Washington, DC, that the federal government could ban slavery from all US territories, and that accused fugitive slaves were entitled to the "privileges and immunities" of citizenship, in particular the rights of due process.

Although he did not openly endorse every one of the many precepts of the antislavery Constitution, Lincoln framed his positions entirely within its parameters. He claimed, for example, that by every principle of law a slave brought into Kansas was free, but he did not cite the Fifth Amendment as a basis for his position. He held that Congress had every right to ban slavery from the territories, but he did not invoke the guarantee clause to make the claim. The founders had compromised with slavery for the sake of creating a Union, but it was a Union they believed would one day be entirely free of slavery. For Lincoln slavery was a temporary, exceptional presence in the Constitution, whereas freedom was perpetual and fundamental.

⟶⟫⟪⟵

BY 1854, when Stephen Douglas engineered the repeal of the Missouri Compromise, the majority of northerners were already inflamed by several years of agitation over the much-despised Fugitive Slave Act of 1850. Among other things, Douglas's bill immediately allowed emigrants from the South to bring slaves into Nebraska territory, from which they had been banned for decades. Primed to respond in outrage to this latest evidence of the increasingly aggressive demands of the southern slaveholders, thousands of northerners poured into the streets in protest.[5] State legislatures passed resolutions denouncing Douglas's Kansas-Nebraska Act, which included the repeal. "Anti-Nebraska" parties sprouted across the North. The Illinois senator acknowledged the furor. He could cross the country, he admitted, by the light of his own burning effigy.

Abraham Lincoln was among those many northerners who were stunned by what Douglas had done. Up to that point in his career Lincoln had been a staunch Whig partisan, generally opposed to slavery but only when the issue arose and not in any meaningful sense an antislavery politician. After leaving Congress in 1849 Lincoln remained active in local politics but devoted most of his time to building up his law practice to support his growing family. The repeal of the Missouri Compromise brought Lincoln back into the center of Illinois politics, where he took the lead in the opposition to Douglas. The senator had scurried home from Washington to salvage his reputation and to hold his fellow Democrats in line. But Lincoln was a Whig and was therefore immune to Douglas's discipline. As the senator stumped across the prairie defending himself in speech after speech, Lincoln took to the road in pursuit, stalking his prey wherever Douglas turned up. In the process Lincoln honed a set of arguments designed to demolish Douglas's self-defense and to offer his own alternative vision of an antislavery Union. The final version of his speech, delivered on October 16, 1854, has come to be known as the Peoria address, after the central Illinois town where Lincoln spoke. It was his first major antislavery

speech, the one that spelled out more fully than any other
the set of policies he endorsed and the antislavery Constitution he invoked to justify them.[6]

Lincoln acknowledged how hard it would be to abolish slavery. "If all earthly power were given me," he said, "I
should not know what to do." He imagined four possible sce-
narios, only the last of which he thought had any hope of
success. "My first impulse would be to free all the slaves, and
send them to Liberia." He referred to the African nation as
the "native land" of southern slaves, as if they were an alien
presence in the United States despite having been here for
generations. Yet however desirable colonization might be,
Lincoln went on, "a moment's reflection" revealed its imprac-
ticality. "If they were all landed there in a day, they would all
perish in the next ten days; and there are not surplus ship-
ping and surplus money enough in the world to carry them
there in many times ten days." So Lincoln's first scenario—
colonization to Liberia—was whisked aside as impractical.
"What then?" he asked.[7]

Lincoln's second scenario was to free all the slaves "and
keep them among us as underlings." It is not at all clear what
Lincoln had in mind here. What would it mean to be free
and yet remain as "underlings"? Whatever he meant, Lincoln doubted that relegating freed people to that mysteri-
ous subordinate status "betters their condition." So that was
out. "What next?" he asked. "Free them, and make them
politically and socially, our equals?" Here Lincoln indulged
in one of his most famous verbal circumlocutions. His "own
feelings" did not allow him to endorse the social and political equality of freed Blacks, but even if his feelings would

allow it, "we well know that those of the great mass of white people will not." He acknowledged that this "feeling" might not accord with "justice and sound judgment," that it might even be "ill-founded." But there was nothing to be done because white opposition to social and political equality was too widespread to be "safely disregarded."[8] Having dismissed the prospect of Black freedom accompanied by either permanent inequality or permanent equality, he returned to his question. What then?

At last Lincoln came to the one scenario he thought realistic, the antislavery policy he could endorse as practical. "It does seem to me," he said, "that systems of gradual emancipation might be adopted."[9] Gradual emancipation was, of course, the "system" that had been adopted in the late eighteenth century by one northern state after another, beginning with Vermont and Pennsylvania and ending with New York and New Jersey. It is sometimes said that in the wake of the American Revolution "the North" abolished slavery. Actually, a number of states abolished slavery, and they came to be known collectively as "the North," or "the free states." This posed a problem. It was all but universally accepted that only states could abolish slavery. Whatever else Congress could do to promote abolition, the one thing it could not do was directly abolish slavery in a state. Nevertheless, there were things the federal government could do to prevent the spread of slavery and encourage the states themselves to abolish it.

At Peoria Lincoln briefly recounted his attempts to abolish slavery in Washington, DC, a position he had endorsed as far back as 1838. He also gave the first indication that he would revise the Fugitive Slave Act to guarantee the due process rights of African Americans in the North who were accused of having escaped from a slave state. As he would throughout the decade, Lincoln denounced the illegal smuggling of slaves into the United States, the suppression of which later became one of his first priorities as president. Finally, and most importantly, he would ban slavery from all the western territories. To Lincoln's way of thinking the territorial ban would do two things. It would rule out any possibility that new slave states would be admitted to the Union, and it would promote emancipation in the older slave states and lead them to adopt gradual abolition statutes on their own. This was the Antislavery Project, invented by abolitionists in the 1820s, endorsed by radical politicians in the 1840s, and adopted in the 1850s by mainstream antislavery politicians like Abraham Lincoln.

As far back as 1821 the pioneering abolitionist Benjamin Lundy published a series of essays on the "Abolition of Slavery" that amounted to the first comprehensive version of the Antislavery Project. Lundy understood that the Constitution did not allow Congress to abolish slavery in a state. Instead he proposed several specific policies that would undermine slavery in a number of ways, short of outright federal abolition. The first policy, the one that would remain central to all later versions of the project, was the abolition of slavery "in all the territories and districts over which congress possesses the exclusive controul." By including "districts" in the proposal, Lundy meant to endorse the abolition of slavery in Washington, DC, as well as the territories. For Lundy the exclusion of slavery from the territories led logically to his next policy proposal, a ban on the admission of any new slave states into the Union. Lundy also proposed a federal ban on the interstate slave trade.

In addition to these policies designed to inhibit slavery's expansion and undermine it in the slave states, Lundy suggested three additional policies to ensure, when taken together, that emancipated slaves would enjoy the opportunity to live wherever they chose. First, he urged the repeal of northern laws that banned the migration of Blacks into the free states. Second, he urged federal subsidies for the voluntary colonization of freed people either to Haiti or to the western territories. Third, he called for the repeal of southern state laws requiring Blacks to leave the state after being emancipated.[10] Abolitionists who came along later would repudiate colonization, whether voluntary or involuntary, because of the increasingly racist cast of the American Colonization Society. But in Lundy's mind, colonization was part of a larger antiracist project, which was in turn part of a still broader antislavery project.

A little more than a decade later, Lundy's protégé, William Lloyd Garrison, and a number of antislavery radicals organized a convention of abolitionists to meet in Philadelphia in 1833 and form the American Anti-Slavery Society (AASS). The delegates endorsed a *Declaration of Sentiments*, drawn up largely by Garrison, which set out the ideology of antislavery nationalism. The radicals asserted that the Union was founded on the principle of universal freedom, that the founders had intended slavery to disappear, but that their revolution had been incomplete. We "cherish, and will endeavor to preserve the Constitution," Garrison and his followers declared, even as they acknowledged the federal consensus: Each slave state "has, by the Constitution of the United States, the exclusive right to *legislate* in regard to its abolition." As "immediatists," the abolitionists declared that every slaveholder had a duty to emancipate his or her slaves *immediately*, "and that the *immediate* abolition of slavery, by those who have the right to abolish it [i.e. the slave states], would be safe and wise." The convention rejected Lundy's endorsement of colonization as part of the larger Antislavery Project, but otherwise AASS would endeavor, "in a constitutional way," to exclude slavery from the western territories, abolish it in Washington, DC, suppress the domestic slave trade, deny any new slave states admission to the Union, and respect the due process rights of fugitive slaves.[11]

The abolitionist Henry Stanton explained the logic of this Antislavery Project. It would steadily increase the number of free states while steadily diminishing the number of slave states. The slave states, increasingly beleaguered and trapped in an unprofitable system, would follow the example of the northern states and, one by one, abolish slavery on their own, beginning in the Border States of the Upper South.[12]

By the time Stanton spoke, the Antislavery Project was already migrating from radical agitation into politics. In 1838 the Massachusetts legislature passed a series of resolutions endorsing an increasingly familiar set of policies, each explicitly grounded in the powers granted to Congress by the Constitution. "Congress has, by the constitution, power to abolish slavery and the slave trade in the District of Columbia. . . . Congress has, by the constitution, power to abolish slavery in the territories. . . . Congress has, by the Constitution, power to abolish the traffic in slaves, between different States of the Union." Finally, Congress should admit no new slave states into the Union.[13]

In 1840 the Liberty Party endorsed a more radical version of the Antislavery Project based on the increasingly robust principles of antislavery constitutionalism. If the Constitution was an antislavery document, William Jay had argued in 1839, it followed that numerous actions taken by the federal government over previous decades were unconstitutional.[14] Hereafter Jay, and the Liberty Party, called for "the absolute and unqualified divorce of the General Government from slavery." The party agreed that slavery would eventually be abolished "by State authority," following the noble example of the northern states. But just as the Northwest Ordinance of 1787 had encouraged five northern states to abolish slavery themselves, so too could a series of federal policies encourage the slave states to follow suit. The Liberty platform was yet another iteration of the Antislavery Project. Congress should abolish the coastwise slave trade, the trade that carried slaves by ship from one slave state to another.[15] Slavery should be abolished in Washington, DC, and excluded from all federal territories. The fugitive slave clause was effectively null and void, an unenforceable exception to the general rule of freedom that was "the true spirit of the Constitution of the United States."[16]

The Free Soil Party of 1848 radicalized the basic precepts of antislavery constitutionalism, even as it narrowed the scope of the Antislavery Project. Free Soilers dropped the defense of the rights of free Blacks that the Liberty Party endorsed, and they limited antislavery policy to its most important element, the ban on slavery in the territories. The platform did not mention either fugitive slave renditions or abolition in Washington, DC. The party's platform asserted that the spirit of the Constitution was expressed in the Declaration of Independence and reflected in the Preamble, which promised "to secure the blessings of liberty." The federal government could not interfere with slavery in a state, but the founders intended to "limit, localize, and discourage slavery" by banning it from all federal territory. Like the Liberty Party, the Free Soil Party called for the divorce of the federal government from slavery "wherever it possesses constitutional power to legislate on the subject." To that end the Free Soilers wanted Congress to ban slavery's expansion into all US territory, thereby preventing any new slave states from coming into existence. "No more slave states and no more slave territory." Because the platform did not mention either fugitive slave renditions or abolition in Washington, DC, it represented a moderation of the Liberty Party's platform. Yet in one respect the Free Soil Party was more radical than its predecessor. It asserted for the first time that the federal government had no power "specifically conferred by the Constitution" to *allow* slavery in the territories. "Congress has no more power to make a slave than to make a king."[17]

The Free Soilers set the pattern that antislavery politicians would follow in the 1850s: expand the scope of antislavery constitutionalism while strategically narrowing the scope of the Antislavery Project to its single most important component. This was Abraham Lincoln's approach. He endorsed the basic principles of antislavery constitutionalism, but despite his personal support of most of the elements of the

Antislavery Project he insisted that for antislavery politics to succeed it had to focus on the one issue most likely to build a winning coalition.

Abolition in Washington, DC

In the first public statement he ever made about slavery Lincoln asserted that Congress had all the constitutional authority it needed to abolish slavery in Washington, DC. He was hardly the first person to say such a thing. James Sloan, a congressman from New Jersey, had proposed District abolition as early as 1805, and ever since the Missouri Crisis abolitionists had petitioned Congress to abolish slavery in the nation's capital. It was part of the Antislavery Project Benjamin Lundy proposed in 1821. Recall that later in the 1820s Congressman Charles Miner, working closely with Lundy, had twice proposed District abolition. But the petition campaign for DC abolition moved into high gear shortly after the American Anti-Slavery Society was formed in late 1833. By the end of 1835 tens of thousands of northerners had signed so many abolition petitions to Congress that southern leaders decided to push back.

In May 1836, a House committee under the leadership of South Carolina representative Henry L. Pinckney reported a resolution that would automatically table all antislavery petitions. Under the new policy the House would take no action on such petitions; they would not even be printed. Pinckney's resolution was the first of the so-called gag rules, and it passed the House by an overwhelming vote of 117 to 68—virtually all the negative votes having been cast by northern Whigs. Pinckney argued that "Congress *ought* not to interfere in any way with slavery in the District of Columbia." On the one hand, Pinckney claimed that slave property was protected by the Fifth Amendment, yet he also seemed to imply that, although it would be imprudent and irresponsible to do so, Congress *could* abolish slavery in Washington. At that point, many of Pinckney's fellow southerners, especially Whigs, were inclined to agree. "On the subject of the right of Congress to abolish slavery in the District," Senator Henry Clay of Kentucky was "inclined to think, and candor required the avowal, that the right did exist."[18] But like Pinckney, Clay thought it highly unwise for Congress to exercise that authority and that abolitionists were impertinent in demanding that Congress do so.[19]

But this was too wishy-washy for the more militant proslavery voices beginning to speak from the South. Henry Wise of Virginia, as well as Pinckney's fellow South Carolinians James Henry Hammond and John C. Calhoun, wanted a firmer assertion that Congress *could not*, under the Constitution, abolish slavery in Washington, DC. Their reasoning was simple. Slaves were a constitutionally protected species of property. "Are not slaves property?" Calhoun asked. "Can Congress any more take away property" than it can deprive citizens of their fundamental rights to life and liberty?[20] It was true, Hammond argued, that the Constitution vested Congress with the power to pass all needful laws for the proper government of the District, but that hardly empowered Congress to violate the Constitution by depriving masters of their property. Antislavery petitions should not even be received,

Hammond claimed, because they demanded that Congress do something it was not constitutionally authorized to do.

Once slavery's defenders shifted the terms of debate to the fundamental property right, abolitionists had to engage the issue at an entirely different level. It was no longer a question of whether Congress, acting on the "needful rules and regulations" clause, *should* abolish slavery in the District of Columbia. Now opponents of slavery had to address the question of whether Congress *could* do so. If the Constitution recognized slaves as property, as the most militant proslavery southerners insisted, Congress *could not* abolish slavery in Washington, DC, because to do so would violate the fundamental rights of property.

Abolitionists responded by going back to first principles and producing a fundamental assault on the right of "property in man." The philosophical starting point for the antislavery critique was the natural right of self-ownership, a right so basic that it could only be taken away by "positive" laws. Since Congress had created slavery in Washington decades earlier when it adopted the slave codes of Maryland and Virginia, it had the same power to abolish it. Indeed, without such a statute slavery could not exist, Henry Stanton argued, because a property right in a human being was incompatible with the underlying premises of the common law, above all the premise that property itself originates in the right of self-ownership. Logically this meant that slavery, not abolition, was the real threat to the rights of property, for slavery "*annihilates*" the slave's property, "not merely his property in his earnings, but in himself." Self-ownership, Stanton declared, was "the sun in the solar system of your rights." Here was a fundamental premise of bourgeois society turned readily into a principled denial of the right of one person to own property in another. "Man's superior right to himself, over the claims of another, is self-evident."[21]

Opponents of slavery moved readily from a defense of the natural right of self-ownership to a critique of the supposed constitutional right of "property in man." In an influential pamphlet defending the power of Congress over slavery in Washington, the abolitionist Theodore Dwight Weld described emancipation as the restoration of the slave's property right in himself and insisted that the "constitution of the United States does not recognize slaves as 'PROPERTY' anywhere."[22] Radical politicians were saying the same thing. In December 1837, William Slade, the fiery antislavery congressman from Vermont, was literally silenced by southern members of Congress who objected to his speech justifying abolition in Washington, DC. Slade reiterated the familiar abolitionist proposition that the right of property originated in the "God-given" right every human has to himself. He flatly denied that the Constitution contained "*a guaranty in favor of slavery.*" What guarantee? Slade asked. "*Where* is it to be found?" Certainly not in the articles protecting private property, he answered, "for, in the first place, the constitution no where speaks of slaves under the denomination of '*private property*,' but as '*persons held to service*.'"[23] Thus did the debate over abolition in Washington clarify the underlying premise of antislavery constitutionalism. Because slavery was not recognized as a constitutionally protected form of property, Congress *could* abolish it in the District of Columbia.

This was the debate that prompted Abraham Lincoln's first public declaration of antislavery sentiments while he was a member of the Illinois state legislature. Angered by the abolitionists' petition campaign, southern legislatures had sent demands to the northern states calling on them to suppress local abolition societies and acknowledge a constitutional right of property in slaves, a right that would be violated by abolition in Washington. The governor of Illinois forwarded the southern demands to the legislature on December 29, 1936, and the state senate appointed a committee to study the matter. A few weeks later each house reported a series of resolutions designed to mollify the South. We "highly disapprove of the formation of abolition societies," the general assembly report began. The "right of property in slaves, is sacred to the slave-holding States by the Federal Constitution. . . . [T]he General Government cannot abolish slavery in the District of Columbia, against the consent of the citizens of said District without a manifest breach of good faith."[24]

The Illinois resolutions are often interpreted as proslavery and, to be sure, they were *designed* to mollify the South. Yet in fact they gave the South nothing. The slave states demanded the suppression of abolition societies; the Illinois legislature merely registered its disapproval of their formation. The slave states demanded recognition of a constitutional right of property; Illinois said only that the right was sacred "in the states" where slavery was legal. The resolutions sent by the slave states claimed Congress had no constitutional right to abolish slavery in Washington, DC. Illinois declared that congressional abolition in the District would be a "breach of faith," not a breach of the Constitution. This may explain why the vote in favor of the resolutions was so lopsided; even antislavery legislators could support them. Nevertheless, Lincoln proposed an amendment to emphasize that Congress *could* abolish slavery in Washington if the residents of the District desired it, but the legislature endorsed the original wording by a vote of 77 to 6. Lincoln was one of the six who voted no.[25]

Six weeks later Lincoln and one other legislator, Dan Stone, issued a "protest against the passage" of the assembly's resolutions "upon the subject of domestic slavery." The "institution of slavery," Lincoln and Stone declared, "is founded on both injustice and bad policy." They agreed that "the promulgation of abolition doctrines" did more harm than good and reaffirmed the federal consensus that the Constitution did not allow Congress to "interfere" with slavery in the states where it was legal. But on the crucial question of congressional power to abolish slavery in the District of Columbia, Lincoln and Stone endorsed the antislavery position. "They believe that *the Congress of the United States has the power, under the constitution, to abolish slavery in the District of Columbia.*"[26] In 1860 the *Illinois State Journal*, widely regarded as Lincoln's journalistic mouthpiece, explained that he had voted against the legislature's resolutions because they reflected "the old Calhoun doctrine" that "the right of property in slaves is sacred to the slaveholding states." This, Lincoln thought, was "abhorrent to his ideas of the true meaning of the Constitution."[27]

Lincoln never wavered from this conviction. On January 10, 1849, while serving his one term in the House of Representatives, he introduced a bill to abolish slavery in Washington, DC. Up until then opponents of slavery had signed petitions and proposed resolutions urging Congress to consider abolition, but Congressman Lincoln went further. His resolution included a complete draft of a bill to abolish slavery in the nation's capital. Though inspired by the gradual abolition statutes passed by northern states during and after the American Revolution, Lincoln's proposal also suggested the influence of the statutes that were used to abolish slavery in the British Caribbean and the Spanish republics of South America. Under Lincoln's proposed bill all children "born of slave mothers" after the bill became law were immediately free, but would serve as apprentices until they reached adulthood. Until then they were to be "reasonably supported and educated" by the owners of the enslaved mothers. To expedite the process, Lincoln's bill offered to compensate masters for the full value of slaves who were born before the law was passed. Like the northern statutes that automatically freed slaves brought into the free states by "sojourning" masters, Section 1 of Lincoln's bill declared the immediate emancipation of all slaves in Washington who were not owned by bona fide residents. The only exceptions were slaves owned by officers of the government from slave states who were in the District working on public business.[28] He would put the bill to a vote of the District's residents, whom he had reason to believe would support it.

Lincoln reaffirmed his position during his famed debates with Illinois senator Stephen Douglas in 1858. "I should be exceedingly glad to see slavery abolished in the District of Columbia," he declared. "I believe Congress possesses the Constitutional power to abolish it."[29] Four years later, as the Civil War entered its second year, the Republican Congress passed and Lincoln signed a bill for the abolition of slavery in Washington, DC. Opponents of the measure once again denounced it as an unconstitutional violation of the Fifth Amendment protection of property. Garrett Davis of Kentucky defied his colleagues to point to the clause of the Constitution that empowered the federal government to take personal property (including slaves) as opposed to real estate.[30] Senator Lazarus Powell, also from Kentucky, agreed. "I regard the bill," he said, "as unconstitutional, impolitic, unjust to the people of the District of Columbia."[31] In signing the bill on April 16, Lincoln rejected such claims. "I have never doubted the constitutional authority of congress to abolish slavery in this District," he explained, "and I have ever desired to see the national capital freed from the institution in some satisfactory way."[32]

Slavery in the Territories

A decade after going on record in support of abolition in Washington, DC, Lincoln publicly endorsed a second piece of the Antislavery Project: a ban on slavery in the western territories. As far back as the 1780s a majority of northern states voted in favor of a bill that would have done the same thing—banned slavery in all the territory then controlled by the new United States. In 1820 a majority of northern congressmen once again endorsed a ban on slavery in all US territory. Nothing had changed when, in the 1840s, a majority of northerners yet again demanded a ban on slavery in all the territories seized in the American war against Mexico.

Well . . . , almost nothing had changed. By then opponents of slavery were starting to claim that Congress not only could ban slavery from the western territories, but that it had a constitutional duty to do so. This was the radicalized version of a long-standing antislavery position, the same version Lincoln himself would adopt.

In 1845 Lincoln wrote a letter to Williamson Durley, a supporter of the abolitionist Liberty Party, making it clear that he opposed the expansion of slavery into the territories. At that point Lincoln's position was relatively moderate. Like Henry Clay, he distinguished annexing the slave state of Texas from allowing slavery into territory where it did not exist. He "never was much interested in the Texas question," Lincoln explained. "I never could very clearly see how the annexation would augment the evil of slavery." He would not object to the migration of slaves into areas like Texas where slavery was already legal, but he steadfastly opposed the introduction of slavery into territories where it had been abolished or had never been legal.

Lincoln's single term in the House of Representatives spanned the very years when the debates over slavery in the territories were reviving the sharp sectional fissure between North and South last seen in the Missouri Crisis. By the time Lincoln arrived in Washington in late 1847 Congress had been deadlocked for quite some time over the Wilmot Proviso, introduced by Pennsylvania Democratic congressman David Wilmot. His proviso would ban slavery from the entire Mexican cession. A majority of northerners in the House consistently supported the ban, but it repeatedly failed in the Senate, where the slave states had more influence. The debates had a familiar ring. Proslavery southerners, led by Calhoun, claimed that slaves were a constitutionally protected "species of property" and as such Congress had no power to legislate on it. Slavery, Calhoun argued, followed the Constitution into the territories. By contrast, antislavery congressmen and senators claimed that Congress could, under the Constitution, abolish slavery in the territories. But by 1848 antislavery congressmen were adopting the more radical antislavery argument that Congress could not constitutionally *allow* slavery into the territories.

Over time Lincoln gravitated toward this more radical position. Several years after leaving Congress Lincoln would claim to have voted dozens of times in favor of the Wilmot Proviso, though it was probably more like five or six times. He never spelled out the constitutional terms on which he cast his vote, but it would have been hard for him to ignore the reasoning of those who cast similar votes against slavery in the territories. The fact that he lived for much of his time in Washington at a boardinghouse famous for its abolitionist residents makes it even less likely that Lincoln was unaffected by the increasingly radical tenor of the debates. But whether he accepted this aggressive antislavery constitutionalism while in Congress or later on, there is no question that by the middle of the 1850s Lincoln subscribed to the view that Congress was morally and constitutionally obliged to ban slavery from the territories, that Congress had—in Lincoln's words—a "duty" to keep slavery out of the territories.

That was the same language used by the Republican Party in the platform it adopted in Philadelphia in June of

1856. Reflecting the antislavery constitutional synthesis of recent years, Republicans linked the ban on slavery in the territories to the right of due process. Because the Fifth Amendment "ordained that no person shall be deprived of life, liberty, or property, without due process of law," Republicans proclaimed, "it becomes our duty to maintain this provision of the Constitution against all attempts to violate it for the purpose of establishing Slavery in the Territories of the United States."[33]

Lincoln acknowledged his party's position. Republicans "believe Congress ought to prohibit slavery wherever it can be done without violation of the Constitution or good faith."[34] But they went beyond a mere assertion that Congress *could* constitutionally ban slavery from the territories. Lincoln was "pledged," he said in 1858, "to a belief in the *right* and *duty* of Congress to prohibit slavery in all of the United States territories."[35] In 1860, the year Lincoln was elected, his party once again invoked the more radical reading of the antislavery Constitution. To "give a legal existence" to slavery in the territories would violate the Constitution's guarantee that no person could be deprived of their liberty without due process of law.[36]

As far back as 1790 Quaker petitioners had implored Congress to undermine slavery "to the full extent of your power." In a sense that became the motto of the antislavery movement. Everyone agreed that Congress could not abolish slavery in a state, but that should not stop Congress from going as far as the Constitution allowed to put slavery on a course of ultimate extinction. In 1855 Lincoln sounded the familiar antislavery refrain when he called on congressmen to "use their utmost constitutional endeavors to prevent Slavery ever being established in any county or place, where it does not now exist."[37]

Fugitive Slaves

Wherever there are slaves there are fugitive slaves. It's always been that way. Slaves ran away in ancient Athens and in antebellum Alabama. There were fugitive slaves in Sicily and in South Carolina, in Benin and Brazil, in Mauritius and Mississippi. But not until slavery became a source of political controversy in the late eighteenth century, when people started debating whether slavery should be abolished, did running away become politically significant. Because some nations clung to slavery while others were abolishing it, international borders began to attract fugitives and soon enough those borders became sources of diplomatic tension. In the new United States of 1787, slavery thrived in some states even as it was being abolished in others. From that moment slaves escaping to free states created a political problem.

The fugitive slave clause of the Constitution recognized the problem, but its intrinsic ambiguity all but ensured that the problem would never be solved. It guaranteed slaveholders a summary right of recaption, but it left the regulation of fugitive slave renditions to the free states. This meant that every slave who escaped from Maryland to Pennsylvania, or from Kentucky to Ohio, opened the possibility of a political conflict between the owner's claim to his or her "property" and the free state's recognition of the accused fugitive's right to due process. To the great consternation of the slaveholders, the northern states exercised their constitutional power to enforce the presumption of freedom within their borders, thereby thwarting the slaveholder's constitutional right of recaption.

In 1842 the Supreme Court issued a ruling in *Prigg* v. *Pennsylvania* that reshaped the terms of the political and constitutional debate over fugitive slaves. To say that Justice Joseph Story's opinion was Delphic is too kind; it was incoherent. It was bad enough that the fugitive slave clause pit the power of free states against the rights of slaveholders. Story's ruling affirmed the slaveholder's right of recaption but transferred primary jurisdiction over contested fugitive slave renditions from the states to the federal government. This made the federal government simultaneously the guarantor of the slaveholders' summary right of recaption *and* the guarantor of the fugitive slave's right to due process. It's no wonder the decision was hailed by some as an antislavery triumph and others as a proslavery disaster.[38]

Under *Prigg* individual states and localities were free to assist in fugitive slave renditions under their police powers, but they were under no obligation to do so. Whether he intended to or not, Story nodded to one of the most distinctive attributes of American legal culture at the time—the enormous discretion police powers gave to local communities. Across the country local officials allowed married women to sue for property rights that the written law formally denied them. Southern localities often heard testimony from Blacks, even slaves, who were statutorily barred from testifying.[39] It was precisely this discretionary police power that enabled so many northern communities to thwart federal fugitive slave

statutes. Aware of this, Associate Justice Roger Taney, despite
agreeing that the federal government was obliged to enforce
the fugitive slave clause, issued a stinging denunciation of
Story's reasoning. If enforcement depended on "the internal powers of police," Taney warned, the Fugitive Slave Act
would not be enforced at all.[40]

Taney had good reason to worry. Across the North
attempts to recapture fugitive slaves were routinely thwarted.
Free Black communities in northern states sheltered runaway slaves from their captors. For decades an alliance of free
Blacks and white abolitionists had been operating an underground railroad that assisted thousands of slaves escaping
from the southern states. To be sure, many northern whites
sympathized with the slaveholders or viewed it as their legal
and constitutional duty to obey the law, but even those who
cared little about slavery were often repulsed by the specter of
slave catchers swarming into their communities and enforcing southern law in northern states. In cities and towns across
the North countless citizens and local police officials refused
to assist in fugitive slave renditions. Northern legislatures
had passed a series of "personal liberty" laws mandating jury
trials and habeas corpus for Blacks accused of being runaway
slaves, mandates the slaveholders considered an assault on
their constitutional right to reclaim their slave property. The
Supreme Court's decision in *Prigg* merely prompted a new
round of state statutes. Some banned state and local officials
from participating in fugitive slave renditions. Others closed
state and local prisons to slave catchers.[41]

To close the loophole Story had opened, in January 1850
Senators Andrew P. Butler of South Carolina and James

Mason of Virginia proposed a new Fugitive Slave Act to replace the statute that had been on the books since 1793. The new law empowered an expanded body of "commissioners," who were little more than clerks, to impose federal authority directly on the North, bypassing obstreperous state and local officials. Slave owners were required to provide only minimal proof of their claims. Accused slaves were explicitly stripped of due process and denied any right to appeal a commissioner's ruling. Commissioners were paid five dollars if they ruled against the slaveholder and ten dollars if they ruled against the fugitive, a common practice designed to account for the extra paperwork involved, but a practice critics denounced as a bribe to encourage rulings in favor of the slaveholder's claim. More disturbing, there was no statute of limitations. African Americans who had built families and worked as free people in the North for decades were vulnerable to re-enslavement at any time. If there were signs of local opposition federal marshals could conscript northern citizens into a posse, forcing them to participate against their wills in the capture and return of alleged fugitives. Three presidents in a row—Millard Fillmore, Franklin Pierce, and James Buchanan—would call out the military to enforce the statute. Heavy fines were prescribed for anyone convicted of helping slaves escape.[42]

Senator William Seward of New York and other opponents of the proposed law warned southerners that it could not be enforced in northern states. Salmon P. Chase of Ohio predicted that the law would "produce more agitation than any other which has ever been adopted by Congress." More curious is the way proslavery southerners pushed for a bill they had reason to believe was unenforceable. Even Butler, the bill's sponsor, admitted that he had "no very great confidence that this bill will subserve the ends which seem to be contemplated by it." This was so not merely because the federal government lacked the means of effective enforcement but, more importantly, because northerners would refuse to enforce it under any circumstances. Robert Barnwell Rhett, the proslavery South Carolinian, questioned the efficacy of a law that clearly contradicted the feelings of the northern community. Jefferson Davis agreed. No matter how powerful the enforcement provisions of the proposed law, it would still be "a dead letter in any State where the popular opinion is opposed to such rendition." He "never expected any benefit to result to us from this species of legislation."[43]

But in the end nearly every southerner in both houses of Congress supported the bill, whereas the overwhelming majority of northern congressmen voted against it or else absented themselves rather than vote for it. In late September, after months of rancorous debate, a slim majority in the House approved it and President Millard Fillmore signed the new Fugitive Slave Act into law. It was one of several bills passed as part of the so-called Compromise of 1850. Party leaders hailed the measures as the "final settlement" of all the controversial issues related to slavery, but that was a fantasy. The hostile northern reaction to the Fugitive Slave Act was as swift as it was severe.

The law provoked a wave of panic in free Black communities across the North. Hundreds of African Americans fled their homes for the safety of Canada. But along with panic came defiance. "I don't respect the law," declared Jermain

Loguen, a Black leader in Syracuse who had escaped from slavery years earlier. "I don't fear it—I won't obey it." Samuel Ringgold Ward, a Black abolitionist, urged Bostonians to make any attempt to enforce the law "the last act in the drama of a slave catcher's life." White allies like Henry C. Wright endorsed Black defiance. If he were a fugitive, Wright told listeners in Cleveland, he would readily "plunge a knife into the heart of his pursuer." Scores of protest meetings erupted all across the North in the weeks and months after the law was passed. Critics denounced these "mongrel gatherings" of whites and Blacks that sprang up in "every city, and nearly every village of the North."[44]

The contentious issue in the politics of fugitive slaves was the law's failure to secure the due process rights of accused runaways. Clay responded to criticism by proposing that jury trials be allowed in the South, in the place from which the slave had escaped, but the slaveholders killed the idea. Seward countered that jury trials had to be convened in the northern communities where the accused was seized; anything else would not guarantee a fair and impartial hearing. William Dayton of New Jersey proposed that "in all hearings before commissioners, depositions had to be authenticated and proof provided that the person claimed was a fugitive."[45] Insisting on extensive documentary proof quickly became another means of thwarting the law. Although accused fugitives were not entitled to advice of counsel, antislavery lawyers appeared at hearings where they grilled slave catchers and demanded verification of the alleged fugitive's identity.[46] In mid-November, only weeks after the 1850 law was passed, the Vermont legislature enacted a statute of its own, guaranteeing accused fugitives a jury trial and habeas corpus. Virginia's governor, John B. Floyd, denounced such "gratuitous intermeddling with our slaves." Vermont's and similar laws were "nothing short of open rebellion and defiance."[47] But given the discretionary police authority of local officials, there was not much slave catchers could do when their efforts were thwarted.

Opponents of slavery came to due process rights for alleged fugitives from various starting points. Traditionally, the common-law right of recaption was self-enforcing; it was up to the masters themselves to find and recapture their slaves with no assistance from government authorities and no process for the captive. But fugitive slave *renditions* were different; they required a legal process that was historically regulated by the states. Salmon P. Chase argued that because the fugitive slave clause lacked an enforcement provision, the Tenth Amendment applied, prescribing that *only* the states could enforce it. Because northern states operated on the presumption of freedom, Chase added, accused fugitives were entitled to due process rights. Radical abolitionists sometimes called for the outright repeal of the fugitive slave clause on the grounds that the summary right of recaption conflicted with the Fifth Amendment right to due process. William Seward considered both the 1793 and the 1850 fugitive slave laws unconstitutional because they violated the due process rights of accused runaways. But whatever the particular logic, all renditions (as opposed to recaptions) required due process rights for accused fugitives.

Lincoln reached the same conclusion by a slower, more moderate route. He did not consider the 1850 statute unconstitutional, nor did he call for its repeal. As a Whig who had always endorsed active government, Lincoln believed—unlike Chase—that the presence of a fugitive slave clause in the Constitution implied a federal obligation to enforce renditions. The question was how to enforce them, and for Lincoln that meant revising the 1850 law to provide due process rights to accused fugitives.

In his first public statement on the issue in 1854, Lincoln said he preferred a statute that "did not expose a free negro to any more danger of being carried into slavery, than our present criminal laws do an innocent person to the danger of being hung."[48] Over the next several years Lincoln mostly bit his tongue, only occasionally repeating his call for revisions to the 1850 statute to remove what he called its "objectionable" provisions—not only the absence of due process protections for accused fugitives but also the obnoxious requirement that northern civilians participate in fugitive slave renditions. Lincoln was never explicit about which due process rights he would extend to accused fugitives: habeas corpus, which opponents of slavery had been demanding since at least the 1780s, or jury trials, which became a rallying cry among abolitionists in the 1830s and was endorsed by many antislavery politicians by the 1850s.

During the early months of the secession crisis Lincoln's position became clearer and more aggressively antislavery. He distinguished the fugitive slave *clause* of the Constitution—which everyone who took an oath of office was sworn to enforce—from the Fugitive Slave *Act* of 1850—which he disliked and wanted to revise. It is important to keep this distinction in mind because Lincoln's commitment to enforcing the Constitution is often mistaken for evidence of support for the 1850 statute. For example, he told John A. Gilmer of North Carolina that he would be happy to see northern states repeal any personal liberty laws that "conflict with the fugitive slave clause, or any other part of the constitution." He told Illinois senator Lyman Trumbull that he favored "an honest inforcement of the constitution—fugitive slave clause included." He told Thurlow Weed that it would be unwise for Republicans to oppose the fugitive slave clause of the Constitution.[49]

At the same time, however, Lincoln called for substantial revisions of the 1850 Fugitive Slave *Act*, revisions that would guarantee the due process rights of accused fugitives. On December 20, 1860, he drew up a set of resolutions he recommended be endorsed by the Republican caucus in Washington. The "fugitive slave clause of the Constitution ought to be enforced by a law of Congress," Lincoln wrote. But unlike the 1850 statute, such a law should not oblige "private persons to assist in its execution," and it should contain "the usual safeguards to liberty, securing free men against being surrendered as slaves."[50] This was Lincoln's most forthright endorsement to date of due process rights for accused fugitives.

Republican leaders met on December 24 to consider Lincoln's proposals. Some continued to believe that the fugitive slave clause should be enforced only by the states, so to maintain party unity Republicans dropped the part of Lincoln's resolution claiming that enforcement was the duty of Congress. But they did endorse the resolution that "the Fugitive Slave Law should be amended, by granting a jury trial to the fugitive." This, Seward wrote Lincoln, "seemed to me to cover the ground of the suggestion made by you."[51] Notwithstanding the differences among Republicans over who should enforce the fugitive slave clause, there was nothing at all unusual about Lincoln's secession winter proposal. The vast majority of antislavery Republicans agreed that the Constitution should be, in Lincoln's word, "honestly" enforced, but in a way that protected due process rights.

Lincoln reiterated his proposal in his inaugural address the following March. "There is much controversy about delivering up fugitives from service or labor," he began. Everyone who swears an oath to the Constitution is of course swearing to uphold the fugitive slave *clause*. The problem was the draconian Fugitive Slave *Act*, which he wanted to replace. "[I]n any law upon the subject," he suggested, "ought not all the safeguards of liberty known in civilized and humane jurisprudence be introduced, so that a free man may not, in any case, be surrendered as a slave?" A proper fugitive slave law should respect the privileges and immunities clause of the Constitution, Lincoln argued, by acknowledging that the citizens of every state were entitled to all the rights of US citizens. So long as the 1850 law remained on the books it should be obeyed, Lincoln said, but there are some laws that communities find so morally offensive that they will never be fully obeyed. The Fugitive Slave Act, he conceded, "was as well enforced, perhaps, as any law can ever be in a community where the moral sense of the people imperfectly supports the law itself."[52] And secession would only make the already lax enforcement of the Fugitive Slave Act even "worse," Lincoln warned, because "after the separation of the sections fugitive slaves, now only partially surrendered, would not be surrendered at all."[53]

With that ominous vow not to return fugitive slaves to seceded states, Abraham Lincoln became the sixteenth president of the United States.

Ultimate Extinction

By the time he was inaugurated president, Lincoln was on record in support of the major principles of the antislavery Constitution. He repeatedly affirmed his commitment to the federal consensus, declaring on several occasions that he had no intention of "interfering" with slavery in the states where it was legal. No less frequently, however, Lincoln denied that the Constitution recognized slaves as property. There was no such thing, he said, as a constitutional right of "property in man." Blacks in the free states and territories were entitled to the presumption of freedom, which necessarily entitled them to the rights of due process. By "every principle of law, ever held by any court, North or South," Lincoln argued, "every negro taken to Kansas is free."[54] Before the Dred Scott decision "courts did have the fashion of deciding that taking a slave into a free country made him free," Lincoln said.[55] He had hoped that the Supreme Court would rule that Dred Scott, his wife, and children "were citizens," Lincoln said, "so far at least as to entitle them to a hearing as to whether they were free or not."[56] Other Republicans offered more robust endorsements of Black citizenship, but it is clear that Lincoln was thinking within the framework of the antislavery Constitution.

Equally consequential for Lincoln was his assumption that the Declaration of Independence was the guiding spirit of the Constitution. Lincoln considered fundamental human equality—the universal right to life, liberty, and the pursuit of happiness—to be "the father of all moral principle" for the government of the United States. Freedom was the rule, slavery the exception. Certain "necessities" had forced the founders to recognize slavery in one or two ways within the Constitution, Lincoln argued, but those concessions did "not destroy the principle that is the charter of our liberties."[57] I am "content with any exception which the Constitution, or the actually existing state of things, makes a necessity," Lincoln explained. "But neither the principle nor the exception will admit the indefinite spread and perpetuity of human slavery."[58] In Lincoln's mind this was the Constitution—the *antislavery* Constitution—the founders had not only written but had written with every intention that it would put slavery on what he called "a course of ultimate extinction."[59]

Of all the policies Lincoln endorsed the one most likely to lead to slavery's extinction was the exclusion of slavery from the territories. Whenever "the effort to spread slavery into the new territories" was "fairly headed off," Lincoln said, "the institution will then be in course of ultimate extinction."[60] Slavery "can only become extinct by being restricted to its present limits, and dwindling out."[61] Excluding slavery from the territories, he believed, acted like "a restrictive fence" that deprived "starving and famishing cattle" of access to food and water.[62] This was known as the "Cordon of Freedom." Surround the South with free states, free territories, and free oceans, and slavery would steadily weaken until the slave states themselves would abolish slavery.

But why would fencing slavery in cause it to die? Lincoln believed that the prosperity of the North was the product of a free labor system that not only rewarded workers with the fruits of their labor but also offered them tremendous opportunities for upward mobility. In the largely rural society in which he was born and raised, upward mobility most often meant that a young man would start his life as an agricultural laborer and end up owning his own farm, eventually hiring laborers of his own. With that kind of freedom and mobility came prosperity. "I wish all men to be free," Lincoln said. "I wish the material prosperity of the already free which I feel sure the extinction of slavery would bring."[63] No slave economy could offer such incentives to workers and generate the prosperity of a free labor economy.[64]

Like so many of slavery's opponents who were convinced of the economic as well as the moral superiority of free labor, Lincoln seriously underestimated the profitability of slavery. He believed that the only way for slaveholders to sustain their profits was for slavery to expand into western territories. Owners in the older, declining, slave states could maintain their profits either by moving themselves to new lands farther west or by selling off their surplus slaves to newly established slave states. Sheer pecuniary interest alone was enough to commit planters to territorial expansion, Lincoln thought. He estimated the slaves, as property, to be worth "a thousand millions of dollars. Let it be permanently settled that this property may extend to new territory, without restraint, and it greatly *enhances*, perhaps quite *doubles*, its value at once." Slaveholders look on their institution "in the light of dollars and cents," Lincoln added, and fully understand that if it were "admitted into the territories," their human property "will have increased fifty percent in value."[65]

By contrast, fencing slavery in would lead to what Lincoln called its natural demise. Although he was never explicit about how that would happen, he apparently accepted the conventional antislavery wisdom that, as the geographically restricted slave economy deteriorated, the slave owners would be driven to free their slaves by the sheer force of economic necessity. Lincoln doubted whether the fate of slavery would be much affected by the annexation of Texas unless, he said, "with annexation, some slaves may be sent to Texas and continued in slavery, *that otherwise might have been liberated*." Here was the critical premise of his opposition to slavery's expansion: It would perpetuate the enslavement of persons who, without expansion, would have been emancipated in the older slave states. "[W]e should never knowingly lend ourselves directly or indirectly, to prevent that slavery from dying a natural death—to find new places for it to live in *when it can no longer exist in the old*."[66] We know that "the opening of new countries to slavery, tends to the perpetuation of the institution," Lincoln observed, "and so does KEEP men in slavery *who would otherwise be free*."[67] Scholars often distinguish opposition to slavery's extension from opposition to slavery itself, but for Lincoln there was no difference. Preventing slavery's expansion led directly to emancipation.[68]

This did not mean that Lincoln rested his hopes on voluntary emancipation by the slaveholders themselves. "So far as peaceful, voluntary emancipation is concerned," the condition of slaves in the South was now "fixed, and hopeless of change for the better," Lincoln complained. "The Autocrat of all the Russias will resign his crown, and proclaim his subjects free republicans sooner than will our American masters voluntarily give up their slaves." Voluntary emancipation may have been fairly common in the early days of the republic, but in recent years many southern states imposed "restraints" on manumission "as to amount almost to prohibition."[69] Abolition would never come about if it relied solely on the voluntary acts of individual slaveholders. They had to be forced into emancipating their slaves by government policies that made slavery economically unsustainable.

Preventing slavery's expansion would increase the number of free states in two distinct ways: state abolition and territorial restriction. As their slave economies deteriorated the southern states would act in their own economic interest by abolishing slavery. Lincoln's model for state-by-state abolition was the northern states where slavery was not strong enough to resist the emancipatory forces inspired by the American Revolution. "Under the impulse of that occasion," he noted, "nearly half the states adopted systems of emancipation at once." Alas, "not a single state has done so since."[70] Instead, westward expansion staved off the inevitable decline that would have led the slave states to abolish slavery on their own, as northern states had done beginning in the late eighteenth century.

Banning slavery from the territories was Lincoln's real-world test case for state-by-state abolition. Without a functioning slave economy, new states coming into the Union would act in their own interest by abolishing slavery in their first state constitutions. In theory there was nothing in the territorial ban that would prevent a state from legalizing slavery as soon as it came into the Union. But in practice, Lincoln pointed out, states carved out of free territories became free states. Thanks to federal exclusion of slavery from various territories, Lincoln explained, the "new year of 1854 found slavery excluded from more than half the States by State Constitutions."[71] For Lincoln state constitutions were the key to abolition. Allow slavery into the territories and "when they come to make a Constitution" the settlers "are obliged to tolerate it in some way." But keep the settlers in the territories "*perfectly* free from the *presence of slavery* amongst them" and later, when time came to adopt a state constitution, "a vote in favor of" slavery "can not be got in any population of forty thousand, on earth."[72] That was the goal of federal policy.

Lincoln thus saw a two-fold advantage in banning slavery from the territories. No new slave states would come into the Union, and the older slave states—deprived of the life support of new territories—would succumb to increasing economic pressure to abolish slavery on their own. Constitutionally, it was the only way slavery could be abolished.

How long would it take for all the states to abolish slavery? Lincoln once speculated that if slavery were abolished in the most peaceful, most gradual way, it would take a hundred years before the last remaining slave finally passed away. It is doubtful that Lincoln believed such a peaceful, gradual abolition was possible. "[T]here is no peaceful extinction of slavery in prospect for us," Lincoln concluded in 1855.[73] "That spirit which desired the peaceful extinction of slavery, has itself become extinct."[74] Still, it's worth asking what he had in mind when he said it would take a hundred years. One way to think about it is to follow the arithmetic of a proposal made by Thaddeus Stevens, the radical Pennsylvania congressman, during the debates over the Compromise of 1850.

If the various elements of the Antislavery Project were put in place by the federal government, Stevens predicted, in twenty-five years the last southern state will have adopted a system of gradual abolition. Surrounded by a "cordon of freemen," deprived of access to new lands in the west, unable to secure their escaped slaves from the northern states, the increasingly isolated slave economies would steadily decline and, one by one, the southern states would gradually abolish slavery on their own. The gradual abolition statutes Stevens referred to generally freed all slaves born after the passage of the law, once they reached adulthood. If the *last* slave born just before the enactment of the *last* abolition statute lived to the age of seventy-five, a hundred years would pass before slavery finally ended—that is, before the last living slave passed away. Of course, by then, millions of slaves would have long since been emancipated.

Stevens's prediction about how slavery would die is probably close to what Lincoln meant by the *most* peaceful, *most* gradual abolition taking a century to complete. But Lincoln did not expect abolition to be peaceful, nor did he want it to take a hundred years. Actually, there's no need to speculate about what Lincoln preferred because he did, as president, make his preferences explicit. In late 1861 he proposed a gradual abolition program for the border slave states that would complete the emancipation process in as few as five and as many as thirty-five years. As always, it was up to the states to decide. By 1863 he accelerated the timetable, suggesting that state abolition be completed in five to ten years. And by 1864 he abandoned gradual abolition entirely. If the states chose to abolish slavery immediately, that was fine with Lincoln. One way or another—gradually or immediately, urged on by the carrot of federal compensation and the stick of federally induced economic necessity—the states would abolish slavery on their own. Meanwhile, slavery having been banned from the territories, no new slave states would have come into the Union. This was "ultimate extinction."

Common Ground

In June of 1858 Lincoln urged his more conservative friend, Ward Lamon, not to run an independent candidate against the radical antislavery congressman Owen Lovejoy. It "will result in nothing but disaster all around," Lincoln warned. Lovejoy, whose brother Elijah had been murdered by an anti-abolitionist mob, was an appealing mixture of high moral principle and political pragmatism—a combination Lincoln very much appreciated.[75] Both recognized that the Republican Party was the best hope for the success of antislavery politics, but both also understood that building an antislavery coalition was no easy task. Lovejoy had a devoted following among some of the most radical antislavery voters in Illinois, and Lincoln saw them as the indispensable base of the party. Republicans could not afford to lose them, which is why he suppressed the anti-Lovejoy insurgency.

But Lincoln also understood that for the Republicans to win they would have to build a coalition of "*strange, discordant, and even hostile* elements"[76]—Democrats opposed only to the extension of slavery into the territories, nativists who were as hostile to Catholic immigrants as they were to slavery, and conservative Whigs repelled by the militancy of antislavery radicals. Lincoln appreciated Lovejoy precisely because he was willing to stand on a "common platform," one that could unite the discordant elements of the young Republican Party. Both men shared an intense desire to craft an antislavery politics that had the broadest electoral appeal. Lovejoy, Lincoln said, was someone "who has been known as an abolitionist, but who is now occupying none but common ground."[77]

The "common ground" of the Republican Party, its broad appeal, consisted of two distinct elements. It pared the Antislavery Project down to its single most important policy—a ban on slavery in the territories—thus appealing to the broadest coalition of voters. But it embedded that one policy in a robust antislavery constitutionalism, thereby appealing to the more radical base of the party. Throughout the 1850s Lincoln never really deviated from his personal support for most of the policies of the larger Antislavery Project: abolition of slavery in Washington, DC, the suppression of slavery on the high seas, and a revision of the Fugitive Slave Act to secure the privileges and immunities of citizenship for accused runaways. But to endorse those policies in the Republican Party platform was to risk alienating some of the very groups Republicans needed to attract. Though he supported abolition in Washington, DC, for example, Lincoln may have considered it a distraction, something that would do little to undermine slavery nationwide but would generate more opposition than was necessary.

Six weeks before the 1858 elections, when he was in the midst of his campaign for the US Senate against Stephen Douglas, Lincoln warned his fellow Illinois Republican Elihu Washburne not to pledge himself "unconditionally against the admission of any more Slave States."[78] It was entirely unnecessary to advocate a ban on new slave states because banning slavery from the territories would inevitably produce only free states. Worse, in Lincoln's mind, it was politically dangerous to advocate such a ban. The following January, in a less anxious tone, Lincoln wrote again to praise a speech recently delivered by Washburne's brother. It was an excellent speech, Lincoln said, well put and well timed. "His objection to the Oregon Constitution because it excludes free negroes," Lincoln added, "is the only thing I wish he had omitted."[79] Yet, a few years later, as president, Lincoln would reject Missouri's constitution on the ground that it contained exactly the same racial exclusion. The point was to build a successful coalition based on the "common ground" of excluding slavery from the territories.

Nowhere was Lincoln more explicit about this electoral strategy than in an 1859 exchange of letters with Salmon P. Chase, the radical antislavery governor of Ohio, regarding the Fugitive Slave Act of 1850. Both men agreed that accused fugitives were entitled to due process, but they disagreed over whether the Constitution left enforcement to states, as Chase believed, or to the federal government, as Lincoln believed.

But the constitutional disagreement was beside the point, Lincoln argued. The issue was that in calling for the repeal of the Fugitive Slave Act, Ohio Republicans were damaging the Republican cause in Illinois. If a plank calling for repeal "be even *introduced* into the next Republican National convention," Lincoln warned, "its supporters and its opponents will quarrel irreconcilably." It would "explode" the party and the convention. The mere mention of repeal was "already damaging us" in Illinois, Lincoln explained, undermining his efforts to win over the more conservative Whigs.[80] His personal commitments notwithstanding, Lincoln believed that the one issue most likely to attract broad support among northern voters was a halt to slavery's expansion, the policy most likely to lead to slavery's ultimate extinction.

But that one crucial policy was contained within a fully developed antislavery constitutionalism, in both the 1856 and the 1860 Republican Party platforms. Scholars like to parse the distinction between the two platforms, often concluding that the 1860 version was more "conservative" than its predecessor. But in their substantive approach to the problem of slavery, they were virtually identical, and on one crucial point the 1860 platform was more radical than its predecessor.

Above all, the Republican Party stood for a policy of excluding slavery from the territories based on an antislavery reading of the Constitution. The 1856 platform summarized that interpretation. The Republicans would restore federal policy "to the principles of Washington and Jefferson." They affirmed the egalitarianism "promulgated" in the Declaration of Independence and "embodied in the Federal Constitution." They cited the "self-evident truth, that all men are endowed with the inalienable right to life, liberty, and the pursuit of happiness." They fused that "truth" to the Constitution's Preamble, its promise to "secure the blessings of liberty" to all, which the platform likewise quoted at length. Securing the fundamental rights of "all persons under its exclusive jurisdiction" was, Republicans declared, "the primary object and ulterior design of the Federal Government." Citing the precedent of the Northwest Ordinance, they claimed that the founders not only abolished slavery "in all our National Territory," they also "ordained" that in that territory "no person shall be deprived of life, liberty, or property, without due process of law." Congress, Republicans declared, had an obligation to protect those due process rights "by positive legislation." By contrast, they would "deny the authority of Congress . . . to give legal existence to Slavery in any Territory of the United States." All of this was true, the platform concluded, "while the present Constitution shall be maintained." That was 1856.[81]

Four years later, the Republican Party platform on which Lincoln was elected president repeated those precepts almost verbatim. The principles of fundamental human equality and universal freedom were embodied in the Constitution. The Fifth Amendment decreed that no person could be deprived of their freedom without due process of law. Congress had no authority under the Constitution to allow slavery into the territories. On the contrary, the Republicans declared in 1860, "the normal condition of all the territory of the United States is that of freedom." They affirmed the federal consensus, "the right of each state to order and control its own domestic institutions." All of that was familiar antislavery constitutionalism. But in 1860 the Republicans went a step further. They denied that "the personal relations between master and servant . . . involve an unqualified property in persons," something they had not said in 1856.[82]

No constitutional right of property in man. Due process for fugitive slaves. The privileges and immunities of citizens for all Blacks in the territories. A Constitution that protects freedom rather than slavery wherever the US government was sovereign. It's no wonder the slave states began to secede from the Union as soon as Lincoln was elected. It was not simply his party's promise to keep slavery out of the territories. Far more frightening to the slaveholders was the increasingly aggressive antislavery constitutionalism, openly and unabashedly proclaimed by Lincoln and his fellow Republicans.

⤜ 4 ⤛

"My Ancient Faith"

Lincoln, Race, and the Antislavery Constitution

I N 1857 Supreme Court Justice Roger B. Taney issued a rul-ing that amounted to a full-throated recitation of the pro-slavery constitutionalism that had been developing over the decades alongside and in reaction to its antislavery counter-part. Nowhere were the irreconcilable differences between the competing Constitutions so fully articulated as in Taney's decision and the dissenting opinions of Associate Justices John McLean and Benjamin Curtis in the case of *Dred Scott* v. *Sandford*. But the Dred Scott decision, and the controversy it aroused, also demonstrated the ways in which the consti-tutional debate over slavery had become inseparable from a corresponding debate over racial equality.

Born a slave in Virginia, Dred Scott was brought to Mis-souri sometime around 1830, where he was sold to John Emerson, a medical officer in the US Army. Scott lived with Emerson for many years while the officer was stationed in both the free state of Illinois and in Wisconsin territory where slavery had been banned since 1820 as part of the Missouri Compromise. During that time Scott married Harriet Robinson and together they had two children. Upon returning to Missouri, Dred Scott, likely at his wife's urging, sued for his freedom on the grounds that he had been liberated by virtue of their residence on free soil. The case dragged on for many years through state and federal courts before landing in the US Supreme Court. In early 1857, shortly after the inauguration of President James Buchanan—who had advance notice of the impending decision—the court ruled against Scott by a 7–2 vote and remanded him and his family back into slavery. Though each of the justices submitted their own opinions, that of Chief Justice Taney was taken to be the opinion of the court.[1]

Taney opened with a long and distorted history purporting to show that Blacks were not and never had been citizens of the United States. They had been brought here as slaves, their enslavement justified by the fact that Blacks were racially inferior, "so far inferior that they had no rights which the white man was bound to respect." Individual states had recognized Blacks as citizens, and historically state citizenship was the basis of "general" or national citizenship. "The citizens of each state," so the Constitution declares, "shall be entitled to all the privileges and immunities of the several states." But Taney broke the constitutional chain that had traditionally tied state and national citizenship, and having done so he ruled that because Dred Scott was not a *United States* citizen he had no standing to sue in federal court. That was all Taney needed to rule against Scott, but rather than stop there he went on to recite the most extreme claims of proslavery constitutionalism.[2]

Scott was not emancipated by virtue of many years of residence in Wisconsin territory, Taney ruled, because Congress had no right to ban slavery in the territory to begin with. He denied the precedence of the Northwest Ordinance. According to Taney, the clause giving Congress the power to make "all needful rules and regulations" for the territories applied only to the territories owned by the United States at the moment the Constitution was ratified and not to any territory acquired thereafter. The Missouri Compromise, which banned slavery in the northern part of the Louisiana Purchase, was therefore unconstitutional. Finally, Taney claimed that "[t]he right or property in a slave is distinctly and expressly affirmed in the Constitution." Thus did Taney attempt to dismantle the basic premises of the antislavery Constitution and in so doing effectively outlaw the antislavery Republican Party.[3]

McLean and Curtis were having none of it. In separate dissents the two associate justices repudiated Taney's botched history and reasserted the major principles of antislavery constitutionalism. Curtis pointed out that when the Constitution was adopted free Blacks were citizens in at least five states, that they even voted for delegates to the ratification conventions. Thus Taney's claim that Blacks were not part of the political community when the nation was founded was historically false. Indeed, under the Articles of Confederation southern congressmen had attempted to restrict citizenship to "free *white* inhabitants" and were voted down by a margin of 10–2. There was no racial qualification for citizenship anywhere in the Constitution, Curtis noted, and no plausible justification for breaking the link between state and national citizenship. "[A]s free colored persons born within some of the States are citizens of those States," Curtis concluded, "such persons are also citizens of the United States." Dred Scott therefore had the right to sue and be sued in federal court.[4]

Having dispensed with the citizenship question, Curtis went on to reiterate the legitimacy of the antislavery Constitution. Congress had every right to ban slavery in the territories and had exercised that right on numerous occasions, Curtis pointed out. He invoked the "municipal" theory, which held that slavery could only exist where positive law expressly sanctioned it. Slaves were not property like any other form of property, as Taney argued, but were recognized as *persons* in divine law, natural law, common law, and in the Constitution itself. Above all, Curtis denied the racial ideology on which Taney's entire opinion rested. The chief justice's claim that "[t]he Constitution was made exclusively by and for the white race" was a mere "assumption" that was contradicted by the Preamble itself. And like the Preamble, the Declaration of Independence promised universal rather than racially exclusive rights.[5]

McLean's dissent was, if anything, a more unflinching defense of the antislavery Constitution. Citizenship was the birthright of free Blacks born in the United States. In the absence of positive law creating slavery, the presumption of freedom prevailed. The needful rules and regulations clause was a general grant of authority to Congress encompassing the power to abolish slavery in all the territories, no matter when those territories were acquired. Indeed, because the Constitution refers to slaves only as *persons*, endowed with all the rights and privileges of persons, Congress has no power to *allow* slavery in the territories. Only in states where enslaved persons were defined as legal property were those constitutional rights overridden. Otherwise the personhood of the slave was not merely constitutional law, McLean argued, it was also higher law. "A slave is not a mere chattel," he argued. "He bears the impress of his Maker, and is amenable to the laws of God and Man." McLean warned that if Taney's reasoning were accepted, if the federal government was obliged to recognize slave ownership as a constitutionally protected right of property, the state laws abolishing slavery could be ruled unconstitutional. Far from constituting the settled law of the land, McLean argued, Taney's opinion was in reality evidence that the reach of the Slave Power extended all the way to the US Supreme Court.[6]

Taney's proslavery Constitution and the competing antislavery Constitution of his dissenting associates represented the judicial reflection of the conflict between slavery and freedom. The same could be said of the political reactions to the Dred Scott decision. Not surprisingly, proslavery southerners embraced Taney's opinion as right and just constitutional doctrine. It was henceforth the obligation of all loyal citizens to defer to the magisterial authority of the nation's high proslavery tribunal. No less surprisingly, Republicans were infuriated. They denounced the decision as "sheer blasphemy . . . an infamous libel on our government . . . a lasting disgrace to the court from which it was issued." The nation's leading Republican newspaper, the *New York Tribune,* granted the decision "just so much moral weight as would be the judgment of a majority of those congregated in any Washington barroom."[7] Preachers, abolitionists, politicians, and editorialists came together in a chorus of denunciation, often openly declaring their defiance of the Supreme Court.

Black activists joined with the overwhelming majority of antislavery northerners to denounce Taney's decision as unconstitutional. Those who accepted Garrison's reading of the Constitution held that Taney's decision was legally correct, however morally repugnant.[8] To Robert Purvis, for example, the Dred Scott decision proved that the Constitution was a proslavery document and that antislavery constitutionalism was "against reason and common sense."[9] But this was a minority view. A Convention of Colored Citizens in Troy, New York,

> Resolved, That the Dred Scott decision is a foul and infamous lie, which neither black men nor white men are bound to respect. . . . We look upon it as an utterance of individual political opinions in striking contrast with the sacred guarantees for liberty with which the Constitution abounds. In order to satiate the wolfish appetite of the oligarchy, Judge Taney and his concurring confederates were obliged to assume that the once revered signers of the Declaration of Independence, and the framers of the Constitution, were a band of hypocritical scoundrels and selfish tyrants. . . .[10]

For the delegates at Troy, the Constitution remained an anti-slavery document, the Dred Scott decision notwithstanding.

In Illinois Abraham Lincoln likewise decried the ruling in terms that closely reflected the opinions of Curtis and McLean, whose dissents had been widely reprinted in pamphlet form. He dismissed most of Taney's decision as *obiter dicta*. It was not "settled" law at all, Lincoln argued; on the contrary, it contradicted long-established precedents. If he were in Congress, Lincoln said, he would vote to ban slavery in all the western territories, despite the court's claim that Congress had no power to do so. In speech after speech Lincoln denied that there was any such thing as a constitutional right of property in slaves.

Taney's decision also relied heavily on the claim that Blacks were not part of the American political community when the nation was founded, that they could not be citizens of the United States, that they had no rights white men were bound to respect. It was therefore impossible for Lincoln to respond to Taney without addressing the issue of racial equality and inequality. If, as antislavery northerners firmly believed, the principle of fundamental human equality was embodied in the Constitution, Taney had to be wrong—not only about the powers Congress could exercise over slavery, but also about the place of African Americans in the history and society of the United States.

In a remarkable speech attacking the Dred Scott decision, Lincoln set out to demonstrate that the chief justice had got his history of African Americans backward. Taney claimed that the condition of free Blacks had steadily improved since the founding era, but Lincoln disputed this. "In some trifling particulars" the condition of Blacks had ameliorated, Lincoln explained, "but, as a whole, in this country, the change has been decidedly the other way." In fact, Lincoln believed, the "ultimate destiny" of African Americans "has never appeared so hopeless." In states where Blacks could once vote, the vote had either been taken away or "greatly abridged," and it had not been extended anywhere. Several southern states now made it all but impossible for individual masters to free their slaves. New state constitutions for the first time denied legislatures the power to abolish slavery. Congress's authority to ban slavery in the territories, once universally accepted, had now been outlawed by the Supreme Court. And the principles of the Declaration of Independence, once "thought to include all," were now sneered at and assailed "to aid in making the bondage of the negro universal and eternal." And still, Lincoln added, the attack on the Black man was growing ever more ferocious. "All the powers of the earth seem rapidly combining against him. Mammon is after him. . . .

> They have him in his prison house; they have searched his person, and left no prying instrument with him. One after another they have closed the heavy iron doors upon him, and now they have him, as it were, bolted in with a lock of a hundred keys, which can never be unlocked without the concurrence of every key; the keys in the hands of a hundred different men, and they scattered to a hundred different and distant places; and they stand musing as to what invention, in all the dominions of mind and matter, can be produced to make the impossibility of his escape more complete than it is.

It was "grossly incorrect," Lincoln concluded, for the chief justice of the Supreme Court "to say or assume, that the public estimate of the negro is more favorable now than it was at the origin of the government."[11] It was worse, immeasurably worse, and Lincoln thought he knew why.

Some Republicans—Owen Lovejoy, Thaddeus Stevens, Charles Sumner—were thoroughgoing racial egalitarians, more so than Lincoln. Others were unabashed racists in a way that Lincoln never was. But the most salient feature of the racial ideology of the Republican Party was its insistence that, when it came to the natural rights of life, liberty, and property, or the privileges and immunities of citizenship, whites and Blacks were fundamentally equal. It is sometimes said that Lincoln's commitment to emancipation was held in check by his racial prejudice, but the evidence suggests something like the opposite. As his immersion in antislavery politics deepened and his commitment to antislavery constitutionalism intensified, it became harder for Lincoln to distinguish his opposition to slavery from his baseline commitment to fundamental equality for whites and Blacks.

Yet if Lincoln endorsed all the equality the Constitution demanded, beyond that his commitment to equal justice for Blacks and whites faltered. Just as the Constitution placed limits on what the federal government could do about slavery in the states where it was legal, so did it leave states free to deny Blacks the right to vote, to marry white people, to serve on juries. Illinois was one such state. It was the home of Stephen Douglas, its most powerful politician, who was also a veritable font of antiblack prejudice. Douglas's authority both reflected and shaped the views of his Illinois constituents. Their elected representatives passed laws designed to prohibit Blacks from moving into Illinois, to keep Blacks off juries, to deny them access to the ballot box, and to prevent Black men from marrying white daughters.

Lincoln, though relatively untouched by racial prejudice, was nevertheless surrounded by it, and he was not above pandering to that prejudice on occasion. But the pervasiveness and increasing intensity of racism among white Illinoisans bred in Lincoln a profound pessimism about the future of African Americans in the United States. Not until the end of his life did he begin to contemplate the possibility of a multiracial democracy. Until then he endorsed—however fitfully and inconsistently—the voluntary colonization of Blacks to some place outside the national borders, a place where they could enjoy the freedom and equality to which they were entitled.

>>><<<

Lincoln said it so often, so clearly and eloquently, that there is no room for doubt: Slavery was wrong because it deprived Black men and women of the natural rights to which every human being was equally entitled. "If the negro is a *man*," Lincoln said in his first major antislavery speech, "why then my ancient faith teaches me that 'all men are created equal;' and that there can be no moral right in connection with one man's making a slave of another."[12] If the Constitution recognized slaves as persons, not property, the Declaration of Independence promised them the fundamental rights to which all persons were entitled.

For saying such things Stephen Douglas and the Democrats repeatedly denounced Lincoln as an abolitionist, a "Black Republican," an advocate of racial "amalgamation." Lincoln in turn condemned Douglas for speaking of Blacks as brutes and animals rather than as men. Douglas would have you believe that those who oppose the enslavement of Blacks are somehow "wronging the white man," that there is a "necessary conflict between the white man and the negro." But there is no such conflict, Lincoln declared in 1859. "I say that there is room enough for us all to be free."[13]

At various points Lincoln questioned the legitimacy of racial categories themselves. Skin color, he warned, cannot possibly justify enslavement because by that rule "you are to be slave to the first man you meet, with fairer skin than your own." Nor would it do to justify slavery on the grounds that whites were intellectually superior to Blacks, for by that rule "you are to be slave to the first man you meet, with an intellect superior to your own."[14] At one point Lincoln blurted out in frustration against the Democrats' obsession with "Negro Equality." "Fudge!" Lincoln declared. "How long, in the government of a God . . . shall there continue knaves to vend, and fools to gulp, so low a piece of demagoguism as this."[15]

Lincoln repeatedly denounced those who claimed that the rights promised in the Declaration of Independence were intended exclusively for whites. The Democrats insisted that Jefferson's ideal was never meant to apply to Blacks, that "the inferior race" should be granted only those rights and privileges "they are capable of enjoying." Lincoln dismissed such reasoning. "What are these arguments?" Turn it "whatever way you will," he said, "whether it come from the mouth of a King, an excuse for enslaving the people of his country, or from the mouth of men of one race as a reason for enslaving the men of another race, it is the same old serpent." Lincoln ended his speech with a plaintive cry for an end to all "this quibbling" over whether this or that race was inferior to the other.[16]

Believing as he did that the natural right to freedom was universal, that every human being was entitled to liberty without regard to race, Lincoln's antislavery argument was at some basic level an antiracist argument; the one made no sense without the other. Short of flatly repudiating the principles of the Declaration of Independence, Lincoln thought, the only way to evade the moral injunction handed down from the founders was to deny what he knew was undeniable— that Blacks were human beings. Conversely, the only way Lincoln could claim that Blacks and whites were equally entitled to their liberty was to assert their equal humanity.

Freedom—liberty—was not the only natural right with which everyone was endowed. Every human was equally entitled to the pursuit of happiness, Blacks no less than whites. This was one of the most important moral precepts developed by enlightenment thinkers in the eighteenth century. Throughout history, they argued, most forms of social organization had deprived human beings of the fruits of their labor and thus left in their wake a protracted legacy of indescribable misery. Societies that robbed humans of what they had rightfully earned by the sweat of their brows paid a steep price for this theft. They destroyed the individual's incentive to work, undermined the general prosperity, and thereby doomed themselves to poverty and famine.

This was more than economically disastrous; it was morally objectionable. Every living man and woman was entitled to a decent life, a modicum of happiness, free from the debilitating effects of poverty and the haunting fear of starvation. Gratuitous starvation—for society is a human, not a divine, creation. It was therefore wrong to organize society in a way that made it impossible for the mass of men and women to rise beyond the destitution that had been humanity's lot for millennia. Here was a moral imperative buried within a classical economic tradition—a tradition that, in other hands, became an amoral justification for indifference to human suffering.[17] The justification for slavery, Lincoln said, was nothing more than an updated version of the ancient argument "that says you work and I eat, you toil and I will enjoy the fruits of it." It came down to a simple proposition: all human beings—Blacks and whites, men and women—were equally entitled to the fruits of their labor.[18]

At the same time, Lincoln distinguished the universal right to freedom from social or political equality. When Stephen Douglas raised the specter of racial "amalgamation" if the slaves were emancipated, Lincoln protested against what he called "the counterfeit logic which concludes that, because I do not want a Black woman for a *slave* I must necessarily have her for a *wife*." He could just "leave her alone," Lincoln explained, adding that although she was "not my equal" in some respects, "in the right to eat the bread she earns with her own hands without asking leave of any one else, she is my equal and the equal of all others."[19] When it came to the natural rights of life, liberty, and the pursuit of happiness, Lincoln was at bottom a racial egalitarian. When it came to the privileges and immunities of citizenship, Lincoln was somewhat less consistent.

→»«←

UNTIL THE Dred Scott decision Lincoln had almost nothing to say about the citizenship rights of free Blacks. But there were hints. When Lincoln said he would have preferred a fugitive slave law that "did not expose a free negro to any more danger of being carried into slavery, than our present criminal laws do an innocent person to the danger of being hung," he was implicitly acknowledging that free Blacks were entitled to the same due process rights as white citizens.[20] This was a weaker endorsement of the citizenship rights of free Blacks compared to other antislavery leaders, but it was far from the denial of Black citizenship increasingly common among proslavery southerners and northern Democrats. On the contrary, Lincoln's tacit acknowledgment of Black citizenship was a reflection of his embrace of one of the basic precepts of antislavery constitutionalism.

The Dred Scott decision nudged Lincoln toward a more forthright defense of Black citizenship. Two weeks after Taney published his ruling Lincoln criticized the chief justice for insisting "at great length that negroes were no part of the people who made, or for whom was made, the Declaration of Independence, or the Constitution."[21] A year later, as he was formulating his thoughts for the upcoming Senate race against Stephen Douglas, Lincoln spelled out what he believed were the elements of a conspiracy to make slavery national and perpetual. "Study the Dred Scott decision, and then see how little even now remains to be done" to make slavery, rather than freedom, national. He reduced Taney's ruling to three major points, the first of which "is that a negro cannot be a citizen." The court's purpose, Lincoln explained, was "to deprive the negro, in every possible event, of the benefit of that provision of the United States Constitution which declares that 'the citizens of each State shall be entitled to all privileges and immunities of citizens in the several States.' "[22]

A few weeks later Lincoln restated his argument at the beginning of his famous "House Divided" speech. Again Lincoln claimed to detect a proslavery conspiracy, a "piece of *machinery* so to speak—compounded of the Nebraska doctrine and the Dred Scott decision." The first of the "*working* points of that machinery" was, once again, Taney's assertion "that no negro slave, imported as such from Africa, and no descendant of such slave can ever be a *citizen* of any State, in the sense of that term as used in the Constitution of the United States."[23] Here Lincoln's commitment to the antislavery Constitution implied a corresponding commitment to some standard of racial equality—not the standard of the twenty-first century, but profoundly significant in a nation where virulent racial prejudice was a significant component of mainstream political culture.

Lincoln anticipated, correctly as it turned out, that his "House Divided" speech would set the terms for his upcoming series of debates with Stephen Douglas. But his response to Douglas revealed the limits of a strictly constitutional equality.

Lincoln says he is opposed to the Dred Scott decision

because it "deprives the negro of the rights and privileges of citizenship," Douglas declared in their very first debate at Ottawa on August 28, 1858. He then unleashed a farrago of racist demagoguery by means of a series of rhetorical questions, all of them aimed at denying the citizenship of free Blacks. "I ask you," Douglas shouted, "are you in favor of conferring upon the negro the rights and privileges of citizenship?" If you "desire negro citizenship, if you desire to allow them to come into the State and settle with the white man, if you desire them to vote on an equality with yourselves, and to make them eligible to office, to serve on juries, and to adjudge your rights, then support Mr. Lincoln and the Black Republican party, who are in favor of the citizenship of the negro."[24] There was no stopping him. "I hold that a negro is not and never ought to be a citizen of the United States," Douglas declared at Jonesboro on September 15. "I do not believe that the Almighty made the negro capable of self-government."[25]

Three days later Lincoln tried to silence his opponent by opening the debate in Charleston with a denial that he had ever supported the social and political equality of Blacks and whites. But Douglas could not be outdone. He shot back at Lincoln with a denial of Black citizenship even more extreme that Taney's. The chief justice had claimed that Blacks could not be citizens because their ancestors had been slaves. But Douglas proudly declared that "a negro ought not to be a citizen, whether his parents were imported into this country as slaves or not, or whether or not he was born here. It does not depend upon the place a negro's parents were born, or whether they were slaves or not, but upon the fact that he is a negro."[26] On and on Douglas went, bellowing forth his denunciations of Abraham Lincoln, the Republican Party, and negro citizenship. Lincoln withered beneath the assault. He pedaled backward, away from any endorsement of Black citizenship rights. "I am not in favor of negro citizenship," Lincoln declared.

He claimed that he had merely stated, as a simple matter of fact, that the Dred Scott decision denied the possibility that Blacks could be citizens, but that he had registered no specific objection to the court's decision. His purpose had not been to endorse Black citizenship but to demonstrate how the decision fit into a larger pattern, a conspiracy, to make slavery national. This was technically true but substantively false. Anyone listening to or reading the "House Divided" speech would reasonably conclude that Lincoln was objecting to the court's decision on Black citizenship, not merely summarizing it. Moreover, it was hard to imagine how Lincoln could embrace the principles of antislavery constitutionalism without thereby acknowledging that the privileges and immunities of citizenship were the birthright of African Americans.

There was more hairsplitting to come. A month later Lincoln gave himself a verbal escape hatch by paraphrasing Douglas's criticism in a curious way. Douglas complains that "I had in a very especial manner" objected to the Supreme Court's ruling on Black citizenship. Not so, Lincoln countered. He had not complained *"especially"* about that part of the decision. He had simply noted it, "without making any complaint at all," along with several other points made in the court's decision. Hence Douglas's assertion "that I made an 'especial objection' (that is his exact language) to the decision on this account, is untrue in point of fact."[27]

Lincoln was running for cover, trying to avoid the virtually radioactive political fallout—certainly in Illinois—from his implicit support for what most northern courts had long since decided: that Blacks were entitled to the privileges and immunities of citizenship, in their states as well as in the nation. On several occasions Lincoln actually did dispute the citizenship ruling, but in a way that seemed calculated not to raise a racist ruckus. He pointed out that under Taney's preposterous rule immigrants who came to America after 1789 could never be national citizens. Nevertheless, Lincoln had learned his lesson. Not until he became president would he dare reopen the issue of Black citizenship.

But reopen it Lincoln did, at the very moment he assumed the presidency. Lincoln inserted into his inaugural address an unambiguous endorsement of Black citizenship rights that could not be misunderstood. As it had in the early 1850s, the issue arose out of the controversy regarding the enforcement mechanisms of the Fugitive Slave Act. Upon taking the oath of office Lincoln reaffirmed the government's constitutional obligation to enforce the law. Nobody disputes this obligation, Lincoln declared, but the issue was *how* it should be enforced. Lincoln would revise the 1850 law in a way that would restore the due process rights of free Blacks in the North. Might it "not be well," Lincoln said, "to provide by law for the enforcement of that clause in the Constitution which guaranties that 'The citizens of each State shall be entitled to all the privileges and immunities of the citizens in the several States?' "[28] Sitting behind Lincoln as he uttered these words were Chief Justice Roger Taney and Illinois senator Stephen A. Douglas. Had Lincoln turned around and slapped both men in their faces his repudiation could not have been more stunning.

What Lincoln hinted at in his inaugural address his administration formally proclaimed a year and a half later. In late 1862, with the final Emancipation Proclamation about to be announced, the citizenship status of the freed people became an urgent question. Lincoln's treasury secretary, Salmon P. Chase, sent a request to Edward Bates, the attorney general, asking whether, as a matter of policy, "colored men [are] citizens of the United States?" Chase's letter was ostensibly prompted by an immediate issue. Federal licensing laws required that all masters of vessels plying the coastal trade be citizens, but many of those masters were Black. If they were not citizens they could lose their licenses. But there was a longer history to Chase's question as well. The same issue had arisen back in 1821 when Attorney General William Wirt published an influential ruling that Blacks were not citizens. Although it was not a judicial decision, Wirt's opinion may have been the most important official ruling on Black citizenship before the Dred Scott case. So Chase was actually asking for much more than an answer to the relatively narrow question of whether Blacks could be licensed or not.

In reply Bates produced an astonishing document, nearly thirty pages long, repudiating everything William Wirt and Chief Justice Taney had to say about Black citizenship. In the first place, Bates ruled, there is nothing in the Constitution that so much as hints at gradations of citizenship, hence there can be no such thing as "full" as opposed to "partial" citizenship. Moreover, the Constitution "says not one word, and furnishes not one hint, in relation to the color or to the ancestral race" of citizens. Every person born on American soil was, "at the moment of birth, prima facie a citizen."[29]

Taney had cited state statutes discriminating against Blacks as proof that they were not considered citizens. This could not possibly be true, the attorney general asserted, for among other things it would mean the laws prohibiting whites from marrying Blacks excluded *whites* from citizenship. But Bates rejected any racial qualifications for citizenship, particularly the claim that Blacks could not be citizens even if they had been born in the country. "As far as the Constitution is concerned, this is a naked assumption," Bates declared, "for the Constitution contains not one word upon the subject." Some people worried that if a Black man could be a citizen he could also become president, but those who objected to Black citizenship on that ground "are not arguing upon the Constitution as it is, but upon what, in their own minds and feelings, they think it ought to be." Anyone who was born on American soil was a citizen, no matter what. Bates thereby restored "birthright" as the basis of "natural-born" citizenship.

But the attorney general went beyond mere restoration in asserting the legal primacy of national over state citizenship. Bates echoed themes first sounded in 1820 by Rufus King and John Taylor, both of whom distinguished rights created exclusively by the states from rights created by the Constitution that applied to citizens everywhere. The privileges and immunities granted to citizens of the United States "cannot be destroyed or abridged by the laws of any particular state," Bates reasoned. On this point, he said, the Constitution "is plain beyond cavil." Citizenship in the United States is "an integral thing"; it cannot be "fractionalized," broken down into parts; it cannot mean one thing in one state and something else in another state. In sum, Bates concluded, Blacks were full citizens of the United States, and the privileges and immunities attaching to their citizenship could not be abridged by the states. And if that were not enough, Bates closed his decision by flicking the Dred Scott decision away like a piece of lint. Once the Supreme Court ruled that Scott was a slave there was no need for the justices to say another word, Bates declared, hence everything Taney had to say about citizenship was "of no authority as a judicial decision."

For all the rhetorical effervescence of Bates's opinion, its practical effect was limited. Antislavery northerners generally considered jury trials, habeas corpus, the right to sue and be sued, to own property, and to travel freely from state to state, to count among the privileges and immunities of citizenship. But Bates did not say that. Like the Constitution itself, the attorney general's opinion failed to specify which rights and privileges free Blacks were entitled to as citizens. Then, too, an attorney general's opinion carries neither the force of statute nor the weight of judicial precedent. As a guide to the principles and practice of the Lincoln administration, Bates's opinion is reliable—it almost certainly reflected the president's thinking—and it did have some effect. Chase's initial inquiry was prompted by a problem that required immediate resolution: there were many African Americans in command of vessels trading along the coast, something they could legally do only if they were citizens. Bates ruled that they were citizens, and the issue was settled. There were also strong indications in Bates's ruling as well as in his diary that the Lincoln administration began issuing passports to Blacks, reversing a decision handed down by a previous administration. But this only exposed how limited the reach of Bates's ruling could be, for the next administration would be as free to overturn Bates as Bates was to overturn his predecessor. Fearing this possibility Congress in 1866 passed a landmark Civil Rights Act, which gave the Bates ruling the force of statute law while spelling out more precisely what the rights of citizenship actually were. At the same time Republicans proposed a Fourteenth Amendment, which completed the reversal of the Dred Scott decision begun by the Lincoln administration.

➤➤❮❮

One of the most important things the Fourteenth Amendment would do was empower the federal government to enforce the civil rights of individuals within the states. Lincoln had always denied any impulse to meddle in matters that belonged rightfully to the states. True, he rejected the extreme state rights dogma that reduced the Union to a mere compact of individual states or that rewrote the Declaration of Independence as though natural rights inhered in states rather than in persons. Still, in every "fragment on government" he jotted down, every passing remark he made about the relative powers of individuals, states, and the nation, Lincoln was careful to respect the rights of states to determine their own "domestic" affairs. "I am for the people of the whole nation doing just as they please in all matters which concern the whole nation," Lincoln explained in 1858, "for those of each part doing just as they choose in all matters which concern no other part; and for each individual doing just as he chooses in all matters which concern nobody else."[30] There were a few obligations, basic but crucial, that belonged to the people as a whole acting through the national government. But some things were best left to individuals, others that were the prerogative of communities, and still others that belonged rightfully to states.

Slavery was typical in this regard. The nation's founding principles condemned it as wrong everywhere, but the Constitution made status conditions the prerogative of states. The status of wives and husbands was prescribed by the laws of marriage in individual states. Indentured servitude was governed by state, not federal, law. Voting rights likewise varied from state to state. So too were states alone free to legalize or abolish slavery.[31] One of Lincoln's objections to the Dred Scott decision was that it allowed masters to take their slaves into western territories "in disregard of the local laws to the contrary." The Supreme Court thereby overturned the long-standing legal principle whereby slavery was "confined to those states where it is established by local law."[32] When Douglas insisted that the states should be free to arrange their domestic institutions however they chose, "including that of slavery," Lincoln's short reply was: "I entirely agree with him." Federal policy should promote the ultimate extinction of slavery, but ultimately the states would do the extinguishing. Lincoln held himself "under constitutional obligations" to allow the people in the states to regulate slavery "exactly as they please."[33]

Among the things states were pleased to do was discriminate against Black people. The principles of fundamental human equality were universal. The privileges and immunities of citizenship were national. But beyond these stood a whole series of "domestic" regulations that had nothing to do with natural rights and were not among the privileges and immunities of citizenship. They included, most importantly, voting privileges, qualifications for officeholding, access to public education, the laws of marriage, and eligibility for jury service. Before the Civil War it was all but universally agreed that such matters were not the federal government's business. Certainly Lincoln agreed. Who could vote, who could hold state office, who could marry whom, who could or could not attend public school, who could or could not serve on juries: these questions were answered in different ways by different state legislatures. In those answers the various states introduced into American law a vast mosaic of racial, ethnic, and gender discriminations. And in deferring to the states on these and other "domestic" matters, Lincoln necessarily deferred to discrimination as well.

If all Lincoln had to say about Blacks was that they were human beings and as such entitled to the same fundamental rights as whites, the case would be closed. But he also said things about race that point in a very different direction. In the same speech at Peoria in which Lincoln first insisted on the irreducible humanity of African Americans, Lincoln also avowed that his "feelings" did not countenance the social and political equality of Blacks and whites. At the opening of the Charleston debate with Stephen Douglas in 1858 Lincoln denied that he had ever been in favor of the social or political equality of Blacks and whites. At a notorious meeting with local Black leaders in Washington, DC, in the summer of 1862 Lincoln suggested that the presence of Blacks was the reason there was a Civil War and asked them to take the lead in urging African Americans to leave the United States.

Lincoln also made dozens of fleeting remarks—including "darky" jokes, occasional use of the word "nigger" (usually paraphrasing someone else), brief statements to the effect that Blacks and whites could not live together as equals—but most of these are too short or ambiguous to support sustained analysis. On a couple of occasions, however, Lincoln said things about Blacks that have become the touchstones for every examination of Lincoln's views on racial equality. They are among the most familiar and disturbing passages in the Lincoln canon.

Lincoln doubted that Blacks and whites could ever live together as equals, but he rarely explained why, much less what he meant. Here and there Lincoln dropped hints about what he was referring to, but he did not specify the forms of inequality until 1858, during his fourth debate with Douglas at Charleston, when Lincoln made the following statement:[34]

> I will say then that I am not, nor ever have been in favor of bringing about in any way the social and political equality of the white and black races, [applause]—that I am

not nor ever have been in favor of making voters or jurors of negroes, nor of qualifying them to hold office, nor to intermarry with white people; and I will say in addition to this that there is a physical difference between the white and black races which I believe will for ever forbid the two races living together on terms of social and political equality. And inasmuch as they cannot so live, while they do remain together there must be the position of superior and inferior, and I as much as any other man am in favor of having the superior position assigned to the white race.

This was Lincoln's single most overt endorsement of racial discrimination, yet several historians have noted the oddly negative phrasing Lincoln used here. He didn't actually say he *supported* the various forms of inequality he listed; he simply said he had never endorsed the several forms of racial equality he specified. He said there was a "physical difference" between Blacks and whites, but he didn't say what the difference was. Lincoln was clearly aware that many people believed those physical differences—whatever they were— necessitated the superiority of whites and the inferiority of Blacks. But Lincoln didn't say whether *he* believed that. What he did say was that as long as Blacks and whites "must be" assigned a position of superior and inferior he would naturally prefer to be "assigned" to the superior category. But who could disagree with that? Who would "favor" being "assigned" to the inferior position?

All of this may be true, but too much time spent on the ambiguities and subtleties of Lincoln's racial misdemeanors begins to sound like special pleading. At the very least Lincoln's remarks at Charleston paid cowardly deference to the racial prejudices of his listeners. A more straightforward reading is also less exculpatory: Lincoln did not support allowing Blacks and whites to "intermarry." He did not support allowing Black men to vote. He did not support allowing Blacks to sit on juries, thereby diluting his commitment to due process rights for accused fugitive slaves. In a state that discriminated against African Americans on explicitly racial grounds, to declare that you'd prefer to be assigned to the superior race is to virtually, if not literally, endorse the racial hierarchy. No doubt Lincoln's defenses of Black humanity and fundamental equality were more consistent, more frequent, and quite unambiguous compared to his periodic bowings and scrapings before the racist peanut gallery. But the contradiction is still there, and it cries out for explanation.

One explanation points to federalism. During his 1858 campaign for the Senate, Lincoln ridiculed Douglas for his obsession with the prospect of Black voters, Black jurors, and racial intermarriage. These, Lincoln said, are state matters, and if Douglas's supporters are so concerned about them they should elect Douglas to the Illinois legislature and send Lincoln to the US Senate. This helps explain a curious disjunction between the fact of Lincoln's racial attitudes and the significance of them.

At Charleston Lincoln specified four areas in which he had never advocated the racial equality of Blacks and whites: voting, serving on juries, holding elective office, and "intermarriage" between whites and Blacks. What these areas had in common was that all of them were regulated by the states. None ranked among the natural rights: few people believed there was a natural right to vote, hold office, marry a white person, or sit on a jury. Nor were they among the traditional "privileges and immunities" of citizenship. None of the discriminations that Lincoln endorsed would deprive Blacks of the right to own or convey property; to speak, publish, or assemble freely; to worship as they chose; or to migrate from one state to another. Blacks might be excluded from the jury box, but they could not be denied the right to trial by jury, the right against self-incrimination, or the right to face their accusers. Nor could Blacks be imprisoned unless formally charged with a crime. Natural rights and the privileges and immunities of citizenship were national, guaranteed by the Constitution to Blacks and whites alike and therefore invulnerable to the wishes of the states. The forms of discrimination that remained, the social and political inequities that Lincoln seemed willing to endorse, were imposed by state legislatures. Freedom was national, the privileges and immunities of citizenship were national, but slavery and racial discrimination were local.

This raises an interesting question. Was Lincoln's apparent endorsement of racial discrimination the product of his prejudice or his commitment to the rights of states? Sometimes Lincoln came close to equating discrimination with state rights. At Ottawa Lincoln denied that in opposing slavery he "was doing anything to bring about a political and social equality of the Black and white races. It never occurred to me," he added, "that I was doing anything or favoring anything to reduce to a dead uniformity all the local institutions of the various states."[35] But the fact that a state could discriminate did not mean that it should. Lincoln would not, for example, endorse the kind of legislation that Massachusetts had recently passed discriminating against immigrants, most of whom were Irish Catholics. Massachusetts had every right to pass the law, he said; it "is a sovereign and independent state; and it is no privilege of mine to scold her for what she does. Still," Lincoln said, "I am against its adoption in Illinois, or in any other place where I have a right to oppose it."[36] So Lincoln openly opposed state laws discriminating against immigrants but registered no similar opposition to state laws discriminating against Blacks.

Racial prejudice is the obvious explanation for the difference, but it is probably not the entire explanation. Lincoln thought a great deal about slavery as a moral, social, and political evil, but he thought very little about race. So his default position on issues of racial discrimination was often deference to popular opinion. Hostility to Catholic immigrants was politically popular in Massachusetts but much less so in Illinois where intense antiblack racism was more widespread. The distinctive patterns of social and political discrimination in the two states reflected the preferences of their respective voters. The racist statutes passed by the Illinois legislature were undoubtedly the will of the state's voting majority, and Lincoln claimed that in a democratic society the racial prejudices of the majority could not be easily disregarded, whether those sentiments were "well or ill-founded."[37] Lincoln may or may not have shared in those popular prejudices but at the very least he was, by his own admission, deferring to them.

Lincoln clearly understood that the racial discriminations he tolerated undermined the ability of Blacks to pursue their happiness and diminished the privileges and immunities of citizenship. "You are cut off from many of the advantages" enjoyed by whites, he said to a delegation of free Blacks in 1863. "The aspiration of men is to enjoy equality with the best when free," he added, "but on this broad continent not a single man of your race is made the equal of a single man of ours." Lincoln had no faith that racial inequality would ever be effaced. "Go where you are treated the best," he told the delegation, "and the ban is still upon you."[38]

For Lincoln, then, there was an unbridgeable gap between the racial equality of natural rights and the privileges of citizenship on the one hand, and a state legislature's right to discriminate against Blacks. Free Blacks could enjoy the rights and privileges of freedom only within the states where they actually lived. When those states imposed a raft of legal discriminations on free Blacks they diminished the meaning of freedom and the value of citizenship. All this Lincoln understood, and yet his solution was not to fight against or even denounce state laws that excluded Blacks from voting and holding elective office. His solution, for too long, was to encourage Blacks to leave the United States, to go someplace where they would be treated as equals.

Nowhere do the contradictions of Lincoln's racial attitudes appear in sharper focus than with his endorsement of colonization. For ten years, from 1852 to the end of 1862, Lincoln periodically advocated government subsidies for the voluntary emigration abroad of African Americans. That said, it was an odd series of endorsements. Sometimes Lincoln raised the prospect of colonization only to dismiss it as impractical. At other times he endorsed the policy while denouncing racists who clamored for it. As president Lincoln encouraged his postmaster general, Montgomery Blair, to develop plans for a colony in Central America, only to toss the contracts in the trash when other members of his cabinet objected. He authorized a payment of about twenty thousand dollars for a privately organized, and for the most part privately funded, project to colonize some five hundred Virginians who volunteered to emigrate to a small island off the coast of Haiti. But Lincoln's most conspicuous role in the scheme was his order to the US Navy to terminate the disastrous project and bring the survivors back to the United States. During the Civil War an unknown number of slaves were colonized by their owners, who carried them off to Cuba or Brazil hoping to evade federal emancipation policy, but in 1862 Congress passed a statute declaring such forced migrations illegal and authorizing the navy to retrieve the slaves and return them to the United States to be freed. Thus Lincoln signed into law a bill that was, in effect, the opposite of colonization. In the end, of the four million slaves emancipated by the war not a single one was deported to a foreign colony by the federal government.[39]

Lincoln had to know why colonization never really got off the ground: It was unpopular. Because colonization presupposed emancipation, opponents of emancipation naturally had no use for it. Among Republicans colonization was extremely controversial. And by insisting that emigration had to be voluntary, Lincoln all but guaranteed that colonization would never overcome the widespread opposition of African Americans. As a policy, colonization was an abject failure.

Why, then, did Lincoln repeatedly endorse it? No doubt

there was an element of political calculation involved. Both before and during the war Lincoln was deeply concerned with building and maintaining a political coalition that included some number of racists—those who wanted to keep not only slaves but all Blacks out of the territories, those who would fight for the Union but not for emancipation. Statements in favor of colonization might appeal to such folks. But when he endorsed colonization Lincoln also had abolition in mind—state abolition. The federal government could not abolish slavery in a state, but it could offer states incentives to abolish it on their own. Compensation was one such incentive. Another was a gradual timetable for abolition. A federal subsidy for the voluntary colonization of African Americans somewhere outside of the United States was one of the incentives Lincoln believed the federal government could offer states to encourage them to abolish slavery on their own.

Lincoln's support for colonization probably had less to do with racism than with racial pessimism. Abolitionists in the late eighteenth century looked optimistically to a future in which emancipated slaves would become full and equal citizens of the United States. But the founding of the American Colonization Society in 1817 reflected a profound shift toward racial pessimism. However halting and inconsistent Lincoln's support for colonization, he shared the ACS's pessimism.[40] He did not believe that whites would ever allow Blacks to live as equals in the United States. As he listened year after year to Stephen Douglas's escalating racial invective, Lincoln could only conclude that the racial prejudice of whites was steadily hardening. Still, in his repeated and at times demagogic endorsements of colonization, Lincoln allowed his racial pessimism to override his commitment to racial equality.

In the late 1850s, however, Lincoln began to discern a connection between southern slavery and northern racism. In a speech at New Haven in March 1860 Lincoln complained that the racism of the northern Democrats was "debauching" public opinion by encouraging Americans to think of slavery as a matter of "indifference." He took particular aim at his arch-nemesis, Stephen Douglas, for claiming that he "don't care" if the people of a state or territory voted slavery up or down. He sensed that the racist demagoguery of Douglas and the northern Democrats was more than a visceral prejudice against African Americans—though it was certainly that. It was also a political strategy designed to undermine the antislavery sentiments of the northern people, to undercut antislavery politics by accustoming Americans to accept slavery as the permanent condition of Black people in the United States.

Lincoln's willingness to attack racial demagoguery grew as his commitment to the antislavery Constitution intensified. If the Constitution was suffused with the spirit of fundamental human equality, if the Declaration of Independence meant anything, it meant that all human beings, Black and white, male and female, had a natural right to be free. For Lincoln southern slavery was doubly incompatible with the Constitution, first because it violated the principle of universal freedom and, second, because it singled out Black people for enslavement.

Unlike colonization, which went nowhere, some of Lincoln's greatest achievements reflected his and his party's commitment to racial equality. The emancipation of four million enslaved African Americans, the enlistment of

Black troops, and the administration's emphatic assertion of Black citizenship—all followed logically from Lincoln's long-standing conviction that Blacks and whites were equally entitled to everyone's natural right to liberty as well as the privileges and immunities of citizenship. The more resolute Lincoln's commitment to undermining slavery, the more committed to racial equality he became, and the more disturbed he was by racist invective. In his last speech defending colonization Lincoln excoriated those who supported the policy simply as a means of ridding the country of Black people. As a young man in the Illinois legislature Lincoln proposed a law that would exclude Blacks from voting. Three decades later, in one of his last speeches, Lincoln became the first president to publicly endorse voting rights for Black men.

→»«←

THE PARADOX THAT limited the reach of the antislavery Constitution had an analog in the limited reach of Lincoln's commitment to racial equality. If, as Lincoln believed, the Constitution was an antislavery document, it nevertheless did not allow the federal government to abolish slavery in a state. Similarly, if the principle of fundamental human equality was embodied in the Constitution, that still left states free to impose any number of degrading discriminations against African Americans. The problem was less ideological than structural. Even the Fourteenth and Fifteenth Amendments proved vulnerable to federalism. With the overthrow of Reconstruction in the late nineteenth century, the promise of equal justice under law succumbed, as did the voting rights of Black men, to the continued determination of states to deprive African Americans of their civil and political rights.

The Thirteenth Amendment was more successful. It did, finally, abolish chattel slavery everywhere in the United States. But the historical pathway that led from antislavery constitutionalism to wartime abolition was a crooked road marked by an unpredictable sequence of events that made the outcome understandable though hardly inevitable.

⊰ 5 ⊱

The Forfeiture of Rights

Emancipation before the Proclamation

None of these rights, guaranteed to peaceful citizens, by the constitution belong to them after they have become belligerents against their own government. They thereby forfeit all protection under that sacred charter which they have thus sought to overthrow and destroy.[1]

William Whiting

It is the old debate continued. The same aspirations, fears, and tensions are there: but they arise in a new context, with new language and arguments, and a changed balance of forces.[2]

E. P. Thompson

ON SEPTEMBER 17, 1859, in a speech at Cincinnati, Ohio, Lincoln warned that if any states seceded from the Union in response to a Republican victory in the 1860 elections the slave owners in those states would forfeit their constitutional right to the recovery of their fugitive slaves. He addressed himself to any Kentuckians who might have been listening that day. "I often hear it intimated that you mean to divide the Union whenever a Republican, or anything like it, is elected President of the United States," Lincoln said. What will you do if a Republican does win, he wondered. Will you split the Ohio River down the middle? "Or are you going to build up a wall some way between your country and ours, by which that moveable property of yours can't come over here any more, to the danger of your losing it? Do you think you can better yourselves on that subject, by leaving us here under no obligation whatever to return those specimens of your moveable property that come hither?" You will have broken up the Union because "we would not do right with you as you think, upon that subject," Lincoln went on, before asking, "when we cease to be under obligations to do anything for you, how much better off do you think you will be?"[3] Secede from the Union, Lincoln warned southerners, and we will no longer be obliged to return fugitive slaves.

Lincoln did not invent the idea. A venerable tradition in Anglo-American law tied allegiance to protection in a reciprocal relationship: to give allegiance to the law was to secure the protection of the law, and to forsake allegiance was to forfeit protection.[4] From that premise abolitionists developed a forfeiture-of-rights doctrine in the late 1830s as part of the broader effort to expand the scope of antislavery constitutionalism. In the face of increasing threats of secession welling up from the South, antislavery northerners argued that any slave state that seceded from the Union would forfeit its claims to constitutional protection of slavery. This was the first of two constitutional principles that shaped the Lincoln administration's earliest moves against slavery.

The second was the emancipatory use of the war pow-

ers clause. Americans had recognized the right of belligerents to emancipate enemy slaves at least since 1784 when they
ratified the Treaty of Paris ending the Revolutionary War.
This may well have been a logical inference from the law of
nations, which justified the confiscation of enemy property
in wartime. But it was not until the 1830s that congressman
and former president John Quincy Adams made a crucial
analytical breakthrough by arguing that the war powers
clause of the Constitution vested Congress with the power
to emancipate slaves if the federal government were called
on to repel a foreign invasion or suppress a domestic insurrection in the slave states. It is important to appreciate these
two precepts of the antislavery Constitution—the forfeiture-
of-rights and the war powers—if we are to make sense of Lincoln's approach to slavery in the first half of the war.[5]

-»>«<-

EVER SINCE THE late eighteenth century the consensus
among American statesmen had been that emancipating
enemy slaves was a legitimate practice under the enlightened
laws of war. This was not surprising because the laws of war
were a subset of the law of nations, and nearly every trea-
tise on the subject held that the law of nations was hostile to
slavery. During both the War of Independence and the War
of 1812 the British freed substantial numbers of slaves who
escaped to their lines, and in both cases the United States
signed treaties acknowledging the emancipation of slaves
"carried away" by British troops before the war ended.

After the War of 1812 John Quincy Adams, virtually

alone, denied that the laws of war legitimized military emancipation. But in 1836 he reversed himself and recovered the legal basis for freeing slaves in the Constitution's war and treaty-making clauses. He did not dispute the federal consensus, but he limited it to peacetime. So long as the slave states "keep within their own bounds," Adams explained, Congress has "no power to meddle" with slavery. But if rebellion or civil war erupted in the South and the slave states appealed for help from the national government, the only legal basis for a congressional response was the war powers of the Constitution. And "when the laws of war are in force, and two hostile armies are set in martial array," Adams explained, "the commanders of both armies have power to emancipate the slaves of the invaded territory."[6] Adams imagined that these war powers would be triggered if the southern states asked for federal assistance to suppress a slave rebellion or repel a foreign invasion. With that, the war powers clause joined the Preamble, the Fourth and Fifth amendments, and the privileges and immunities clause as one of the mainstays of antislavery constitutionalism.

Adams's speeches were widely reprinted, and by the mid-1850s there was general agreement among Republicans—from the most radical to the most conservative—that secession would lead to war and war would lead in turn to emancipation. In 1856 the relatively conservative Francis Preston Blair warned of "the fatal effects" of the dissolution of the Union on the security of "the slave institution." It was "well known," Blair argued, "that civil war, in a nation where slavery exists, liberates the slaves."[7] Two years later, in 1858, Joshua Giddings, the antislavery radical from Ohio, cited "a principle understood by all intelligent men that when war exists, peace may be obtained by the emancipation of all the slaves held by individuals, if necessary."[8]

No Republican leader expressed the conviction that war led to emancipation more consistently than William Seward. As early as 1825 a young Seward confidently declared that "the south will never, in a moment, expose themselves to a war with the north, while they have such a great domestic population of slaves, ready to embrace any opportunity to assert their freedom and inflict their revenge."[9] Later, as a senator from New York, Seward repeated his prediction on several occasions, including his famous "higher law" speech of 1850. He posited a stark distinction between gradual abolition in peacetime and immediate emancipation in wartime. Threats of southern secession posed the all-important question of "whether the Union shall stand, and slavery, under the steady, peaceful action of moral, social and political causes, be removed by gradual, voluntary effort, and with compensation, or whether the Union shall be dissolved, and civil wars ensue, bringing on violent but complete and immediate emancipation."[10] Seward made the same point at Auburn, New York, in 1855. "Slavery is not, and never can be, perpetual," he declared. "It will be overthrown, either peacefully or lawfully, under the constitution, or it will work the subversion of the constitution, together with its own overthrow. Then the slaveholders would perish in the struggle."[11]

In January 1861, in one last futile attempt to forestall secession, Seward once again warned that war would destroy all hope of a gradual, peaceful abolition. He repeated the warning he had first issued in 1825, that in a civil war the

millions of slaves would not remain "stupid and idle specta-
tors." The United States had pioneered a path toward peaceful, gradual abolition, one state at a time, whereas European
nations—presumably Britain, France, and the Netherlands—
had imposed "simple, direct abolition, effected, if need be, by
compulsion" in their Caribbean slave colonies. The attempt
to dismember the Union would bring European-style abolition to the United States. The only "umpire" for secession
was war, Seward warned, and in that case "what guarantee
shall there be against the full development here of the fear-
ful and uncompromising hostility to slavery which elsewhere
pervades the world?"[12] What John Quincy Adams had once
presented as abstract doctrine, the incoming secretary of
state threw down as a direct threat.

By then Republicans had also adopted a second precept of antislavery constitutionalism, the forfeiture-of-rights
doctrine, which would have a direct bearing on Lincoln's
response to fugitive slaves from the earliest weeks of the war.
In 1839 the New York abolitionist William Jay developed the
idea in an influential tract called *A View of the Action of the Federal Government, In Behalf of Slavery.* Adams had argued that
war would empower the federal government to interfere with
slavery within the slave states themselves. But Jay argued that
secession, with or without war, would relieve the northern
states of any obligation to enforce the fugitive slave clause of
the Constitution. Although primarily concerned with expos-
ing the long history of federal support for slavery, toward the
end of his book-length essay Jay turned his attention to the
various ways the federal government could inhibit slavery
without violating the constitutional rights of slaveholders.

Those rights were secure, Jay argued, only if the slave states remained in the Union, whereas secession would "deprive the institution [of slavery] of the protection of the Federal Government." Should the slaves rise in rebellion in a seceded state their masters could not call on the "fleets and armies" of the republic for assistance. "And by what power would the master recapture his fugitive who had crossed the boundary of the new empire?" Jay asked. *Within* the Union the slaveholders were entitled to recapture fugitives "through the whole confederacy." But as soon as the slave states left the Union, "freedom would be the boon of every slave who could swim the Ohio, or reach the frontier line of the free republic." Secession, moreover, would aggravate "the anti-slavery feelings of the North," leading the free states to "afford every possible facility to the fugitive" by passing laws "not for the restoration of human property, but for the protection of human rights."[13]

Radical antislavery politicians like Horace Mann were soon rehearsing the forfeiture-of-rights doctrine on the floor of Congress. Secession, Mann warned, would metaphorically move the Canadian border down to the Ohio River, absolving northerners of any obligation to return fugitive slaves from disloyal states. But the argument was not the sole preserve of antislavery radicals. Lincoln, as we've seen, warned in Cincinnati in 1859, and again in his inaugural address in March 1861, that seceded states would forfeit their constitutional right to the return of their fugitive slaves. The threat first made by the abolitionist William Jay a generation earlier had clearly entered the mainstream of American politics and was enshrined in Lincoln's first speech as president.

Meanwhile in Congress Republicans responded to secession by invoking the specter of John Quincy Adams and the emancipatory force of the Constitution's war powers clause. In late January Republican congressman John A. Bingham, citing Adams, warned that the "first blast of war" would be "the trumpet signal of emancipation." Congressman James Ashley likewise argued that the federal government, "once involved in war," could undertake "*the removal, by force if necessary, of the cause that produced the rebellion*." This, he added, "is no new doctrine," for John Quincy Adams had spelled it out "nearly twenty years ago, in the House of Representatives."[14] Ashley and Bingham were radicals, and there is no doubt that radicals were particularly enthusiastic about the prospect of military emancipation. But military emancipation was not confined to radicals; it had long been accepted by American statesmen and mainstream Republicans. Before the first battle of the Civil War was fought, the conservative Republican Orville Browning said the same thing. "Whenever our armies march into the southern states," Browning declared, "the negroes will, of course, flock to our standards.—They will rise in rebellion, and strike a blow for emancipation."[15] Thus by the time the Civil War began, Adams's constitutional doctrine was widely accepted among antislavery politicians across the North.

Within weeks of the Confederate bombardment of Fort Sumter, Lincoln implemented the forfeiture-of-rights doctrine by directly authorizing a Union general in Virginia to refuse to return fugitive slaves to their owner. Two months later, on July 13, Congress authorized the president to issue a proclamation declaring a state, or any part of a state, to be

in "insurrection." Thereafter all "goods and chattels" coming into the United States from an area in rebellion shall "be
forfeited to the United States."[16] Two weeks after that Congress authorized the permanent forfeiture of slaves escaping to Union lines from rebellious masters and the Lincoln
administration, acting on the president's war powers as commander in chief, emancipated the forfeit slaves.

From those early beginnings Lincoln's antislavery policy would evolve over four years of war into an increasingly
radical assault on the institution of slavery, culminating in a
constitutional amendment abolishing slavery everywhere in
the United States. The forces propelling that evolution were
many—among them the fortunes of the competing armies
on the battlefield, the pressures of diplomacy, and not least
the determination of slaves to take advantage of the war to
emancipate themselves.

Yet it would be a mistake to see the radicalization of emancipation policy as the inexorable working out of the intrinsic
logic of the antislavery Constitution. What if the slaves had
not run to Union lines? What if Kentucky seceded? What if
the Confederates secured the high ground on the first day
at Gettysburg and Lee went on to crush Meade? What if the
British recognized southern independence? What if the radical Republicans had not been so effective in steering federal
policy? What if the Republicans lost control of Congress in
1862, or Lincoln lost to McClellan in 1864? What if the Thirteenth Amendment failed to squeak through the House of
Representatives in January 1865? The path to wartime abolition was strewn with contingencies.

What mattered, no less in the Civil War than at any other

great turning point in human history, was the way men and women responded to those contingencies. In 1861, as slaves began running for freedom to Union lines, President Lincoln and congressional Republicans reacted in ways consistent with their long-standing commitment to the antislavery Constitution. Influenced as well by the fugitive slave crisis of the 1850s, Republicans constructed their first antislavery policy on the assumption that slaves would activate it by escaping to the invading Union army. They called the policy "self-emancipation."

Contrabands vs. Fugitives

Before the war the fugitive slave clause of the Constitution decreed that "persons held to service" who escaped to a free state could not thereby be "discharged from service," that is, emancipated. Slaves who succeeded in escaping to the North and establishing new lives for themselves were still, legally, fugitive slaves subject to the threat of recapture. Shortly after the war began, however, slaves could free themselves from disloyal states or disloyal masters by escaping to Union lines where they were emancipated as a matter of federal policy. In the first year of the war such slaves ceased to be fugitives; they became, instead, contrabands.[17]

For the policy makers, the crucial issue was disloyalty. At the heart of the first wartime emancipation policy was the premise that disloyal states and disloyal masters from loyal states forfeited their right to their fugitive slaves. As of May 30, 1861, slaves coming voluntarily within Union military lines or into Union territory from states and masters in rebellion were deemed "contraband of war" and would not be returned to their owners. As of August 8, 1861, contrabands were emancipated. But emancipation did not apply to "fugitives from service," those who escaped from loyal owners in one of the four loyal slave states—Delaware, Maryland, Kentucky, and Missouri. Such slaves fell under the legal rubric of the fugitive slave clause of the Constitution.

On May 23, 1861, three slaves escaped from their owner to the Union military base at Fortress Monroe, in Virginia. The next day their owner's representative showed up to demand that the slaves be returned, in accordance with the Fugitive Slave Act of 1850. Major General Benjamin Butler, who had just arrived from his previous assignment in Maryland, refused the owner's request on the ground that "the Fugitive Slave Act did not affect a foreign country, which Virginia claimed to be." With secession Virginia masters had forfeited their constitutional right of recaption. Butler would therefore retain the escaped slaves as "contraband of war." By contrast, Butler added, "in Maryland, a loyal State, a fugitive from service had been returned."[18] At Fortress Monroe Butler was prepared to return those first three escaped slaves to their owner if the owner swore an oath of loyalty to the Union. But as the owner was manifestly disloyal, Butler deemed his slaves "contrabands" rather than "fugitives" and would not return them. Thus the distinction between "contrabands" and "fugitives from service" was, as it were, present at the creation of federal emancipation policy, and at the core of the distinction was loyalty to the United States.

Butler immediately wrote to his superiors in Washington informing them of his action and asking them to endorse his refusal to enforce the Fugitive Slave Act in a disloyal state. President Lincoln called a special meeting of his cabinet on May 30 to consider Butler's request, and at the conclusion of the meeting Secretary of War Simon Cameron informed the general that his contraband policy "is approved."[19] Barely six weeks after the surrender of Fort Sumter the Lincoln administration had taken the critical first step toward a policy of military emancipation. To be sure, slaves who escaped to Union lines from rebellious owners were not yet emancipated, but neither were they returned to their owners: they were instead retained as contraband of war. As General Butler had indicated, because Virginia seceded from the Union the slaveholders from that state had forfeited their claim to the return of escaped slaves.

Butler objected in principle to the idea that human beings could be owned as property. But as southern masters claimed slaves as their legal "property" under state law, Butler turned the tables on them by labeling the fugitives "contraband" and thus liable to confiscation under the laws of war. This was an unorthodox use of the concept of "contraband of war," which under international law had traditionally referred not to enemy property but to goods shipped to an enemy by a third party. Nevertheless, Butler's label proved instantly popular and, more importantly, it established the categorical distinction between contrabands and fugitives that would shape Union emancipation policy for the rest of the year. Butler reiterated the distinction on June 29. "In a loyal state, I would put down a servile insurrection," he explained. "In a state of rebellion I would confiscate that which was used to oppose my arms."[20] It was a fairly simple principle, but an essential one: Slaves escaping from loyal owners in loyal slave states were legally "fugitives from service," whereas slaves escaping from disloyal owners or from states in rebellion were "contraband of war."

The new contraband policy was widely reported in the press, and word of the distinction between loyal and disloyal states spread quickly among masters, slaves, and Union soldiers. "It seems to be understood that the Maryland fugitives can be regained by their masters," a Washington newspaper reported, "but the Virginia masters may have to wait a while."[21]

The difference between the legal status of escapees from the two states created new opportunities for enslaved Marylanders. Numerous reports suggest that slaves escaping from Maryland began flocking into Washington, DC, where, despite their legal status as "fugitives from service," they were difficult to distinguish from the far more numerous "contrabands" coming in from Virginia. Legal "fugitives" from Maryland, aware of the policy, sometimes claimed they were "contrabands" from Virginia. In November A. D. Harrell, commander of the USS *Union*, reported that "some forty or more contrabands" had taken refuge on several naval vessels. "I have no doubt that many of them are from Maryland," Harrell wrote, "notwithstanding they invariably represent themselves as coming from Virginia."[22]

The Lincoln administration's policy of not returning "contrabands" to their owners did not mean that federal officials were suddenly committed to the aggressive capture and return of legal "fugitives." As we have seen, the Fugitive Slave Act of 1850 was practically a dead letter across much of the North, as whites and Blacks found legal and extralegal ways to evade the statute. There was no reason to believe that after years of resistance and systematic nonenforcement northerners, particularly the antislavery politicians who were now in control of the federal government, would suddenly begin enforcing laws they had long denounced and evaded.

The question of *who* should enforce the fugitive slave clause had been a major source of contention before the Civil War, but there was nothing in either the Constitution or the 1850 statute that gave military personnel the authority to decide whether a Black person who showed up at Union lines was free or enslaved. Although a Democratic administration had argued several years earlier that the president could order the military to enforce the Fugitive Slave Act, that opinion was widely disputed.[23] By the time the war began it was a commonplace among Republican policy makers that the US military had no business participating in the capture and return of fugitive slaves. Not surprisingly, military officials made nonenforcement the de facto policy of the federal government, especially when it concerned US military personnel. In their dealings with fugitive slaves of loyal masters in loyal slave states, Union soldiers would be— in the parlance of the day—neither slave catchers nor slave emancipators. That was nonenforcement.

Federal nonenforcement rested on the well-established distinction between fugitive slave *renditions*, which required a legal process in the free states, and the master's common-law right of recaption, which was technically self-enforcing. For all practical purposes, rendition hearings in the free states came to an end during the Civil War and federal emancipation policy reverted to the right of recaption. By tradition this meant that masters in search of fugitive slaves were on their own; they could expect no help from government officials. "In these cases of fugitive slaves and fugitives from justice," a New York judge had declared in 1835, "it is not certain that any legislation whatever is necessary, or was contemplated by the framers of the Constitution."[24] Two years later the widely respected attorney James C. Alvord published an influential essay in the *American Jurist* arguing for a strict construction of the fugitive slave clause. "The clause is perfect in itself," Alvord argued, "and works its own object."[25] No congressional enforcement statutes were called for, much less constitutionally justified. William Seward argued that when confronted by slaveholders demanding the return of their fugitives, the proper response of northerners should be *go get them yourself.*

As far back as the 1830s army officers sometimes refused to participate in fugitive slave renditions on the grounds that they lacked the judicial qualifications and authority to determine whether any individual was slave or free. This hands-off approach persisted into the Civil War. When the war began, Republican lawmakers insisted that the military was not empowered to enforce the Fugitive Slave Act. Often when loyal masters showed up at Union camps demanding the return of their escaped slaves, the official response was *go ahead and look for them but don't expect our soldiers to assist you.* In a single case early in the war, Lincoln appears to have relied on the principle that loyal masters were responsible for capturing their own fugitive slaves.

Sometime in late June of 1861 Caroline Noland, a loyal owner from Rockville, Maryland, complained to federal authorities that one of her slaves had fled to Washington, DC, and made his way to a Union army camp occupied by the First and Second regiments of Ohio. From there the fugitive accompanied the soldiers across the Potomac River to Camp Upton, in Virginia. Noland and her sons repeatedly attempted to recover the alleged fugitive but failed to do so either because the slave was no longer in the camp or because soldiers were hiding the fugitive from the slave catchers (as the owners suspected) or because Noland made the whole story up and never owned such a slave to begin with, as one of the Union officers suggested.

Frustrated in her initial attempts to recover her slave, Noland brought her complaints to higher-ups in the War Department, one of whom accused the Ohio troops of "practicing a little of the abolition system in protecting the runaway."[26] Brigadier General Robert C. Schenck angrily denied the charge and insisted that "persons owing labor or service to *loyal* citizens of *loyal* States if they resort to us shall always be surrendered when demanded on proper order or authority by the lawful owner or his representatives."[27] Schenck would not return the slaves of disloyal owners from disloyal states; he would surrender legal fugitives—slaves escaped from loyal masters in loyal states—but only under direct orders to do so and only to owners or legal representatives who had come on their own to retrieve the runaways. Nevertheless, Schenck implied that in some limited circumstances his soldiers might assist loyal masters from loyal states, but that did not help Mrs. Noland.

She appealed unsuccessfully to the secretary of war and at least three assistant adjutant generals. Faced with obstreperous Union soldiers and obstructionist federal bureaucrats, she next turned for help to Maryland congressman Charles B. Calvert, who took up her cause in a letter to President Lincoln on July 10. Union soldiers in Washington were not only employing fugitive slaves from Maryland in their camps, Calvert complained, "but have actually transported them with them into Virginia."[28] Calvert demanded that such fugitives be returned, thereby creating a problem for the president.

Two days before Calvert wrote his letter Lincoln told Illinois senator Orville H. Browning that "the government neither should, nor would send back to bondage such as came to our armies."[29] The next day, July 9, the Republicans in the House of Representatives all but unanimously endorsed Owen Lovejoy's resolution declaring that "it is no part of the duty of the soldiers of the United States to capture and return fugitive slaves."[30] As we have seen, this was standard antislavery doctrine. Among Republican congressmen it was a simple matter to point out that under the 1850 Fugitive Slave Act federal commissioners and marshals, not Union soldiers and sailors, were authorized to enforce fugitive slave renditions. As for the slaveholder's right of recaption: that remained self-enforcing. What Congressman Calvert was asking Lincoln to do clearly went against the wishes as well as the legal understanding of most Republicans.

Lincoln's response was to acknowledge, though reluctantly, the right of recaption by which the loyal owners from loyal states could retrieve fugitive slaves on their own. He wrote to Lieutenant General Winfield Scott asking whether it would "not be well to allow owners to bring back those which have crossed" the Potomac—"crossed," that is, from the loyal state of Maryland to the disloyal state of Virginia. But even going that far was sufficiently embarrassing to the president that he asked that his name not be mentioned in the instructions. So when Scott relayed Lincoln's suggestion to Brigadier General Irvin McDowell he made it clear that "the name of the President should not at this time be brought before the public in connection with this delicate subject." McDowell immediately instructed the assistant adjutant general to "take stringent measures to prevent *fugitive slaves* from passing over the river particularly as servants with the regiments ordered over."[31] Although the president's request was issued through the military chain of command, Lincoln was careful not to order Union soldiers to search for and return slaves who were still legally "fugitives from service." Instead, Lincoln merely asked whether *the owners of the slaves* should be allowed to find and recover the fugitives.

The Noland incident was a side effect of the policy of refusing to return contrabands to their owners, a reversal of the prewar policy of using US troops to enforce fugitive slave renditions. Before the war, when Maryland slaves attempted to escape, they headed northward to the free states, sometimes hoping to follow the North Star. But in June 1861 Maryland slaves suddenly reversed course and began heading for the Potomac, "passing over the river" into the seceded state of Virginia. Why? And why would Union soldiers in Washington, DC, perhaps "practicing a little of the abolition system," bring Maryland slaves with them as they crossed the

Potomac into Virginia? Because as of May 30, 1861, fugitives from Maryland and soldiers from Ohio knew about the policy adopted by the administration—that slaves entering Union lines from the disloyal state of Virginia were presumed to be contrabands rather than fugitive slaves.

Yet for several months there was no federal policy of emancipating contrabands. Congress was out of session through May and June of 1861, when the contraband policy went into effect, and the legislators would not return to Washington until early July. As soon as the special session of Congress opened, however, several Republicans introduced bills that resulted in the passage of the First Confiscation Act on August 6, 1861, legalizing the permanent confiscation of slaves used in support of the rebellion.

In drafting the statute Republican lawmakers drew directly from the language of the fugitive slave clause of the Constitution, which referred to slaves as "persons held to service," and said they could not be "discharged from service" if they escaped to a free state. The new law used the same wording but reversed its implications by invoking the language of forfeiture. Any disloyal master who employed a "person held to service" in support of the rebellion "shall forfeit his claim to such labor."[32] Lincoln believed that Congress could not emancipate a slave in a state until the slave had first been confiscated and ownership was transferred to the United States. Under the First Confiscation Act the slaves of disloyal masters were permanently confiscated but not emancipated. But Republicans had no intention of making the federal government the owner of confiscated slaves. And so on August

8, two days after Congress had authorized the forfeiture of slaves used in support of the rebellion, Lincoln's secretary of war issued the instructions to *emancipate* them.

The War Department instructions confirmed that the distinction between contrabands and fugitives hinged on loyalty. All slaves escaping from disloyal areas—contrabands—were emancipated, unlike "fugitives from service" who escaped from loyal areas. "[N]o question can arise as to fugitives from service within the States and Territories in which the authority of the Union is fully acknowledged," the secretary of war explained. In loyal areas the federal government could not violate the rights of slaveholders that were protected by the Constitution. "But in the States wholly or partially under insurrectionary control, where the laws of the United States are so far opposed and resisted that they cannot be effectually enforced, it is obvious that rights dependent on the execution of those laws must, temporarily, fail." Rights "dependent on the laws of the States"—such as the right of property in slaves—must be "subordinated" to military needs "if not wholly *forfeited.*" Even more clearly than the congressional statute, the War Department invoked the precise wording of the fugitive slave clause, only to reverse its effect. The War Department declared that "persons held to service" and used in support of the rebellion "shall be forfeited *and such persons shall be discharged therefrom.*"[33]

With that, the Lincoln administration began emancipating slaves, or in the language of the Constitution, discharging them from service. As of early August 1861 Lincoln's policy was to emancipate all slaves who came within Union lines from areas in rebellion or rebellious masters, whereas slaves who escaped from loyal owners in loyal slave states remained "fugitives." But the fine legal distinction proved all but impossible to implement in practice, especially in a city like Washington, DC.

The Blue Jug

With the wide publication of Butler's contraband policy and the May 30 administration endorsement, a growing number of contrabands fled into the District of Columbia in the summer of 1861 only to discover that local police and unsympathetic Union soldiers were still arresting fugitives and contrabands alike and housing them in the Washington, DC, jail known as the Blue Jug. The jail was built in 1839 to accommodate about eighty prisoners, but slave owners and traders soon began using it as a holding pen for slaves pending sale or for fugitives who had escaped to the city hoping to find freedom by blending inconspicuously into the city's free Black population.[34] By 1860 the jail was seriously overcrowded and badly in need of renovation. Inspectors had repeatedly called on Congress to replace the Blue Jug with a new facility, but Congress never appropriated the necessary funds. Conditions inside the jail worsened in the summer of 1861 as the city's wartime population swelled with raucous Union soldiers, common criminals, contrabands from Virginia, and fugitives from Maryland. James Grimes, the antislavery Republican who chaired the Committee on the District of Columbia, complained that the city jail was being "perverted from the uses for which it was erected" and "was being used for private purposes, and as a means of oppression." Grimes appealed to Secretary of War Simon Cameron and on July 4, 1861, Cameron ordered the release of all the prisoners. On the same day the military commander in Washington, Joseph K. Mansfield, instructed city officials to enforce the administration policy. Fugitive slaves coming into Washington from Virginia should be considered "as contraband" and "shall not be returned to the rebellious owners."[35]

In August Republicans replaced the notoriously pro-slavery police officials in Washington, DC, with men who, it turned out, were scarcely more sympathetic to escaping slaves. Together with local constables and justices of the peace, the police continued to arrest Blacks whether they were fugitives from Maryland or contrabands from Virginia. Soon stories of the scandal at the Washington jail were making their way into the national press. By December there were reportedly 235 prisoners jammed into the Blue Jug, three times as many as the facility was designed to hold. About one hundred of the prisoners were Black, and of those approximately sixty were being held as runaway slaves. In early 1862 a congressional committee issued a scathing report denouncing management of the jail which, the committee concluded, "presents features of wretchedness more deplorable than a civilized people could desire for their worst culprits."[36] Inmates were routinely beaten. The prisoners were nearly starving because the federal marshal, Ward Lamon— one of Lincoln's cronies—pocketed most of the funds used to feed them, as had Lamon's predecessors.

In late 1861 the provost marshal for the district hired Allan Pinkerton to investigate, and as soon as the new

congressional session opened in early December Massachusetts senator Henry Wilson placed a summary of Pinkerton's
scathing report in the Congressional Record. Pinkerton
focused on the illegal detention of those held as runaway
slaves. Some were free Blacks who had come to Washington
as servants of Union army soldiers. Others had escaped from
"disloyal masters" serving in the rebel army. Some had been
captured "by the faithful minions of slavery and disloyalty"
while working for the Union army. Pinkerton contrasted
the disloyalty of the masters and captors with the loyalty
of the imprisoned Blacks. They often came into Washington with intimate knowledge of the condition of the rebel
armies as well as "the conduct and whereabouts of disloyal
persons within our lines." Pinkerton suggested that "these
sixty unfortunate 'contrabands' . . . be set at liberty, under
the protection of the provost guard, to engage in the numerous useful and remunerative situations open for them, in the
city." He was not suggesting that all sixty slaves be emancipated. "Those not found strictly 'contraband,' or free, can be
otherwise disposed of after examination." The report thus
recognized the implicit distinction in federal emancipation
policy. Just under fifty of the slaves were legally "fugitives
from service" whose final disposition remained uncertain.
Twelve others, "strictly contrabands," were therefore "free."
Wilson introduced the report in support of a resolution calling for the release and employment of *all* the slaves.[37]

Pinkerton also recommended that the local officials who
were arresting contrabands should themselves be arrested,
a recommendation Lincoln quickly endorsed. On the same
day that Wilson introduced the Pinkerton report, Secretary

of State William Seward, acting on Lincoln's instructions, ordered Major General George B. McClellan to punish any civil or military official who violated the administration's contraband policy. "Persons claimed to be held to service under the laws of the State of Virginia," Seward explained, "frequently escape from the lines of the enemy's forces and are received within the lines of the [Union] army of the Potomac." Such persons coming into the city of Washington "are liable to be arrested by the city police, upon the presumption, arising from color, that they are fugitives from service or labor." This was a clear violation of federal policy. Seward pointed out that under the terms of the First Confiscation Act slaves used in service of the rebellion and escaping into the city "are received into the military protection of the United States, and their arrest as fugitives from service or labor should be immediately followed by *the military arrest of the parties making the seizure*." Contrabands from Virginia were free upon entering the city, and any civil or military authorities attempting to arrest them as "fugitives from service" would themselves be arrested.[38] Seward sent official copies of Lincoln's order to the mayor of Washington and to Lamon, the federal marshal. Within days the warden released all sixty slaves being held in the jail.

Seward's order is yet another example of an antislavery principle developed before the war and applied directly to wartime conditions. As far back as the 1780s northern states had passed anti-kidnapping laws that imposed fines and jail terms for anyone attempting to carry Blacks into a slave state. In 1850, in response to the southern demand for a stringent new fugitive slave law, Seward himself proposed an alterna-

tive amendment that would subject judges and police officials who violated the rights of accused fugitives to heavy
fines and loss of employment. "Any judge or magistrate who
shall disallow such a writ of habeas corpus," Seward's amendment read, "shall forfeit to the person claiming it, five thousand dollars, and shall also forfeit his office; and any marshal
who shall unreasonably hinder or prevent such person from
suing out or serving such writ of habeas corpus, shall, in like
manner, forfeit five thousand dollars and forfeit his office."[39]
Eleven years later Seward ordered the Union army to arrest
any civil or military official who attempted to seize a fugitive slave who had escaped into Washington, DC, from a disloyal state.

In January 1862, a month after the controversy over
conditions in the Blue Jug flared up, Lincoln ordered the
release of the slaves who were legally "fugitives" but who had
ended up in the jail. Lincoln believed that because the federal government was the exclusive enforcer of the fugitive
slave clause, federal officials were therefore free to establish
the procedures by which it was enforced. He had long before
endorsed the standard antislavery position that accused fugitives were entitled to the rights of due process. Acting on that
premise Lincoln ordered Secretary of State Seward to issue a
new set of rules for dealing with fugitives in the Washington,
DC, jail. Like the northern personal liberty laws that closed
state and local prisons to slave catchers, Lincoln's order
decreed that the Blue Jug could no longer be used "to receive
slaves for safe keeping." Nor could actual fugitives be held
for extended periods of time, another long-standing practice
that had sometimes resulted in the sale of slaves unclaimed

by their owners. Instead, the marshal was ordered to "discharge from custody at the end of thirty days" any "fugitives from labor" who had not been "lawfully reclaimed by their owners."[40]

By early 1862 the porous border between the loyal state of Maryland and the seceded state of Virginia, with the nation's capital situated between them, had led Lincoln and various members of his cabinet to issue a series of orders, instructions, and reports, all of them tending in the same direction: fugitive slaves escaping from disloyal states or owners should not be returned by anyone operating under the authority of the federal government.

Missouri and Kansas

Like the Maryland-Virginia boundary, the border slave state of Missouri presented geographical conditions that clarify Lincoln's emancipation policy. Although Missouri was one of the four slave states that remained loyal to the Union, a substantial portion of the state's economic and political elite was openly disloyal. With assistance from the Confederacy, secessionists in Missouri organized their own military force, and by the summer of 1861 a civil war within the Civil War had divided the state into loyal and disloyal regions. As events spun out of his control, Union general John C. Frémont responded on August 30 with a proclamation declaring that the property "of all persons in the State of Missouri who shall take up arms against the United States . . . is declared to be confiscated to the public use, and their slaves, if any they have, are hereby declared freemen."[41] At the very least this was a poorly worded proclamation. Congress had mandated the permanent confiscation of all slaves actually used in the rebellion, and the administration had extended that to include all slaves coming into Union lines or Union territory from rebellious areas or owners, at which point they were emancipated. Lincoln's policy had created a structural opportunity for the slaves to emancipate themselves; it worked only if slaves voluntarily came within Union lines or into Union territory. Frémont's proclamation did something different. It applied to all owners in a vast area of a loyal slave state and it purported to free all their slaves even though they were far removed from Union lines and had little opportunity of escaping to freedom. In effect, Frémont violated federal policy by removing the slaves' agency from the emancipation process.

A few days after Frémont issued his proclamation Lincoln asked the general to "modify" it so that it conformed to the first and fourth sections of the First Confiscation Act. Lincoln "perceived no general objection" to Frémont's order; he merely asked that it be rewritten to conform to the law. In an extraordinary response the general refused to comply with the request of his commander in chief, telling the president he would not modify his proclamation unless "you will openly direct me to make the correction." Lincoln reiterated that his concern with the emancipation clause of Frémont's proclamation was "it's non-conformity to the Act of Congress," the First Confiscation Act. He "therefore ordered that the said clause of said proclamation be so modified, held, and construed, as to conform to, and not to transcend" the congressional statute.[42] Generals cannot be allowed to make policy, especially not when the policy openly violates a congressional statute. That, Lincoln said, is "military dictatorship." Frémont's order, Lincoln complained, "assumes that the general may do *anything* he pleases—confiscate the lands and free the slaves of *loyal* people, as well as disloyal ones."[43] Strictly speaking, this was a misreading of Frémont's proclamation, which applied to those who had taken up arms against the Union. Nevertheless, Lincoln's order to Frémont, far from demonstrating that his administration had no emancipation policy, affirmed the policy of emancipating the slaves of disloyal owners, even in a loyal slave state.

Frémont's proclamation was in many ways an act of desperation by a political general whose arrogance and military incompetence were rapidly becoming obvious. It did not help that his administration was monumentally corrupt. Dubious contracts for "shoddy" cloth and worthless muskets were common enough in the early months of the war, but the Western Department under Frémont was notorious for the scale and sheer brazenness of corruption. Congress opened an investigation in July and by September the evidence was already voluminous. Frémont overruled inspectors who had proof that the general's cronies were skimming huge profits from the sale and resale of army supplies that had already been rejected as unacceptable. Frémont's own wife, Jessie Benton Frémont, was known to accept "gifts"—a horse and carriage—from hopeful contractors. In October inspectors discovered that of the 411 "cavalry" horses purchased by the army in St. Louis—Frémont's headquarters—330 were unfit for service. Five of the horses were already dead.[44] On October 24, Lincoln finally removed the general from command.[45] The point is not that Frémont was uniquely corrupt, but that his fate was sealed not by his emancipation edict but by his military ineptitude and the mounting evidence of massive fraud compiled by the congressional committee.

Upon firing Frémont the president immediately appointed David Hunter to replace Frémont in western Missouri.[46] In his letter of instruction Lincoln advised Hunter to cooperate with General James H. Lane, commander of the Kansas Brigade, a US Army unit that had in recent months been raiding western Missouri and emancipating thousands of slaves. Hunter arrived in Missouri in late November and the two men met at St. Joseph, after which Lane gave a "characteristic speech" to soldiers from the 16th Illinois Infantry Regiment, vowing to suppress the rebellion by destroying its cause—slavery.[47]

Lane was a fascinating character who played an outsized role in the development of federal antislavery policy during the earliest months of the Civil War. A veteran of the violence that had spread through Kansas in the 1850s, when "border ruffians" from Missouri tried to force a proslavery constitution on the antislavery majority of settlers, Lane came away from that experience with a seething hatred of both slaveholders and slavery. He served briefly as the first senator from Kansas in 1861, during which time he gained notoriety as an outspoken supporter of military emancipation.[48]

While in the Senate, for example, on July 18 Lane reacted furiously to a resolution introduced by Lazarus Powell, the proslavery senator from Kentucky. Powell would have Congress declare that neither the Union army nor the Union navy should be "employed or used . . . in abolishing or interfering with African slavery in any of the States."[49] Lane quickly subverted Powell's proposal by adding an emancipation amendment to the anti-emancipation resolution. The Union military could not interfere with slavery in the states, Lane's revision declared, "except to crush out rebellion or hang traitors." Lest anyone wonder what Lane was up to, he made himself absolutely clear. "I do believe," Lane said, "that the institution of slavery will not survive, in any State of this Union, the march of the Union armies, and I thank God that is so."[50] A few weeks later, when the special July session of Congress adjourned, Lane secured an appointment as a Union officer, resigned his seat in the Senate, and headed home to take command of the recently organized Kansas Brigade.

By October Lane was putting his emancipationist principles into practice, leading his troops in a series of raids from Kansas into the pro-secession slaveholding counties of western Missouri. Thousands of Missouri "contrabands" proceeded to abandon their masters and follow Lane's troops back into Kansas, where they were emancipated. "The Federal troops here take every negro they can lay their hands on," one slaveholder complained, "whether he belongs to a Union man or a secessionist. They have negroes in their army, too, equipped as white soldiers—In short, their manner of proceeding here is enough to disgust any decent white man."[51] On October 21 newspaper reports from St. Joseph told of "a continual flight of 'contrabands' from this city Kansas-ward." One Black preacher was said to have "[m]ysteriously vanished from the vision of his rebellious master," only to turn up a few days later, across the state line, preaching the gospel in Leavenworth, Kansas.[52] In November a correspondent for the *New York Times* witnessed similar activities. "Day before yesterday, Lane sent back to Kansas 100 negroes, and this morning, as his train passed, I counted 102 more of these ebony chattels."[53] Governors, mayors, and Democratic papers across the country were soon denouncing Lane. But when he gave militant antislavery speeches the crowds cheered Lane on and his troops took to calling him "the Liberator."

Lane responded unapologetically to the complaint that his troops "steal slaves." In a speech in Leavenworth, in late October, he freely admitted that one of his own officers "has just returned from the interior of Missouri, and they tell me he comes back with more slaves than white men." Adopting the antislavery principle that the military was not responsible for enforcement of the Fugitive Slave Act—that the slave owner's right of recaption was self-enforcing—Lane insisted that if the masters were loyal they would not be molested in their attempt to recover their slaves, but neither would they receive any assistance from any Union soldiers. Loyal owners, not Union soldiers, would be responsible for the capture and return of their fugitives. "Secessionists," on the other hand, "get no slaves from the Kansas brigade," Lane declared. "Is there a man here who would act as a slave catcher . . . ? This is the sin, this is the charge against us. *We march to crush out treason, and let Slavery take care of itself.*" Slavery "disappears before my brigade," Lane admitted. "I guess that's true."[54]

Having been in Congress and participated in the debates over the First Confiscation Act, Lane knew precisely what federal emancipation policy was and therefore understood how to implement it within the administration's guidelines without violating the congressional statute. Unlike Frémont, Lane issued no proclamations declaring the emancipation of slaves in areas over which the Kansas Brigade had no control. Instead Lane preserved the principle of self-emancipation, making slaves agents in their own liberation. Yet his actions led to the emancipation of far more Missouri slaves than Frémont's would have or could have. Justifying his behavior, Lane reminded his listeners in Kansas of what he had promised while in the Senate. "I stated in Washington that the institution of slavery could not survive the march of the Federal army," Lane declared, "*that there would be an army of one color marching into the slave states and an army of another color marching out.*"[55]

Strictly speaking, Lane insisted, he would not make war on slavery. The proximity of his troops would create the opportunity for slaves to emancipate themselves, but he would neither entice slaves from their owners nor "steal" slaves from secessionists. When he said that "slavery will take care of itself," that it would not survive the march of Union armies, Lane meant that his troops would do nothing to prevent the slaves from taking advantage of the war by coming to Union lines and claiming their freedom, that his soldiers would treat such slaves as contrabands who had emancipated themselves. Yankee troops would passively withhold assistance from loyal masters seeking to recapture their fugitive slaves, but they would actively prevent secessionist owners from reclaiming emancipated contrabands. By December thousands of enslaved Missourians had freed themselves by following Lane's troops into the free state of Kansas.

Lincoln removed Frémont from command at the end of

October, just as reports of Lane's doings began appearing in the eastern press. Yet the president's response to the two generals could hardly have been more different. Having fired the corrupt and incompetent Frémont, Lincoln promoted Lane to brigadier general and appointed an abolitionist general to oversee Lane's command in western Missouri. Shortly thereafter, in early December, Lane left on a trip back to Washington, where he would meet with Lincoln at the White House. Along the way, the irrepressible Lane continued to give militant speeches denouncing slavery and vowing to destroy it. "We can have no permanent peace except in the extinction of slavery, the cause of the war," Lane told an audience in Syracuse.[56]

Announcing Administration Policy

Even as Lane made his way back east in December of 1861, a flood of reports, proclamations, and announcements poured forth from the administration, making it clear that the Kansas Brigade was merely implementing the emancipation policy that had been in place for months. On December 3, in his first annual report to Congress, the president himself invoked the forfeiture-of-rights doctrine that had long since become a staple of antislavery constitutionalism. Under the terms of the First Confiscation Act "the legal claims of certain persons to the labor and service of certain other persons have become *forfeited*," Lincoln declared, and the slaves were "thus liberated."[57] It cannot have been an accident that on the very next day, December 4, Lincoln instructed Secretary of State William Seward to publish his order for the arrest of any military or civil authorities who violated federal policy by attempting to seize "contrabands" in the District of Columbia.

Seward was not alone. Three more cabinet secretaries elaborated on the administration's emancipation policy in their separate annual reports. On December 1, Secretary of War Simon Cameron declared that in wartime belligerents have the right "to subdue the enemy, and all that belongs to the enemy." In the rebel states the principal source of wealth and power "is a peculiar species of property, consisting of the service or labor of African slaves." Why, Cameron asked, "should this property be exempt from the hazards of a rebellious war"? Rehearsing the familiar forfeiture-of-rights doctrine, Cameron went on to claim that "[t]hose who are against the Government justly *forfeit all rights of property, privilege, or security, derived from the Constitution.*" Accordingly, "the slave property of the South is justly subjected to all the consequences of this rebellious war."[58] Had he stopped there Cameron's annual report would have gone out without notice.

But Cameron then proposed that liberated slaves be armed and enlisted in the Union army. This would have violated the Militia Act of 1793, which restricted enrollment to free white males. At that point Lincoln was still reluctant to enlist Blacks in the army, and in any case he believed that it was up to Congress to change the law (which it did the following July). He therefore ordered Cameron to revise the wording. "The important alteration consists in cutting out the secretary's proposition to arm the slaves," the Springfield *Republican* reported. "In regard to the employment and freedom of the slaves coming within our lines, the president agreed with Mr. Cameron."[59] So did others in Lincoln's cabinet.

Two more secretaries affirmed the "employment and freedom" of the slaves in their first annual reports. Both revealed the Republican Party's underlying assumption that achieving "freedom" resided in large measure in the transition from slavery to wage labor. As far back as May, General Butler had justified his refusal to return fugitive slaves on the ground that they were willing to work for the Union in return for wages. But where in the spring Butler could only retain slaves as "contraband," by late summer they were also emancipated. Treasury Secretary Salmon P. Chase's annual report of December 9 explained that persons held to service as slaves under state laws were "justly liberated from their constraint" when they came within Union lines. But rather than simply hold them as confiscated property, Chase reasoned, the former slaves could be made "more valuable in various employments, through voluntary and compensated service."[60] Chase's report is particularly significant because at that point slaves who came within Union lines were transferred to the authority of the Treasury Department; hence, the secretary's defense of "voluntary and compensated" labor represents the most authoritative statement we have of the administration's policy in December 1861. A few months later the treasury secretary made the policy abundantly clear to a South Carolina planter who asked about the status of his slaves who had come within Union lines. "They were free," Chase told him.[61]

Chase was not alone either. Navy Secretary Gideon Welles noted in his annual report that along the southern coast "fugitives from insurrectionary places have sought our ships for refuge and protection." The policy of the Navy Department, Welles explained, was that the fugitives "should be cared for and employed in some useful manner, and might be enlisted to serve on our public vessels or in our navy yards, receiving wages for their labor." If the navy had no job to offer, the fugitives "should be allowed to proceed freely and peaceably without restraint to seek a livelihood in any loyal portion of the country."[62] By the end of the first year of the war the administration had adopted wage labor as the alternative to slavery for contrabands coming within Union lines.

Like all policies, however, this one was not uniformly implemented wherever the Union forces showed up. For individual slaves there were countless different routes to freedom, many of them circuitous. Throughout the war Union advances and reverses sometimes resulted in emancipations followed by re-enslavements with Confederate reoccupations, followed by further emancipations. Yankee soldiers were as divided over emancipation as were Yankee voters, and there were always some soldiers who turned contrabands over to their owners.[63] One of them was Charles W. Stone, a brigadier general and proslavery Democrat who was excoriated by congressional Republicans for returning fugitive slaves to their owners in late 1861. It was bad enough that soldiers who returned slaves were ignoring federal policy, but Republicans also assailed such soldiers for disregarding the Constitution. Charles Sumner denounced Stone for his "vile and unconstitutional" behavior. Worse, Stone ordered his soldiers, against their will, to participate in the "discreditable and unconstitutional" business of capturing and returning fugitive slaves. Sumner urged Congress to pass "additional legislation that our national armies shall not be employed in the surrender of fugitive slaves."[64]

Edgar Cowan, one of the most conservative Republi-

cans in Congress, replied that such legislation was unnecessary because soldiers in the field had no legal authority
to enforce fugitive slave renditions. An ordinary soldier was
not equipped, much less empowered, to decide the case of
a master who came to a Union camp demanding the return
of someone he claimed was his slave. Cowan then rehearsed
the legal logic of nonenforcement. When a master comes
to a Union camp claiming his fugitive slave, the Union sol-
ider must reply, "No; you cannot do that" because "that pre-
sumes that I decide the very question I am incompetent to
decide." Meanwhile, the only thing the president could do,
in his capacity as commander in chief, was emancipate the
slave. The war powers clause of the Constitution already gave
the president the power to free enemy slaves, Cowan pointed
out. Slavery was perfectly legal in peacetime, he said, but
when the peace is broken "the fetters fall from the slave."[65]

This was the unassailable principle Stone had violated by
returning fugitives to their owner, and for that reason Republicans in Congress decided to make an example of him. They
hauled Stone before the Committee on the Conduct of the
War, which recommended his imprisonment. Secretary of
War Edwin M. Stanton agreed, and Stone was sent to jail for
six months.

More confounding than soldiers who openly violated
Lincoln's policy was General Henry W. Halleck, who tried
to square the government's self-emancipation policy with his
belief that civilians should be excluded from army camps.
On December 4, 1861—the same day Seward ordered the
arrest of anyone attempting to seize contrabands on the
streets of Washington, DC—Halleck issued "General Orders

No. 13," excluding slaves from military camps. Acknowledging the policy already in place, Halleck conceded that the laws of the United States "confiscate the property of any master in a slave used for insurrectionary purposes."[66] And in recognition of Congress's objection to the use of the army to enforce the Fugitive Slave Act, Halleck chastised officers who assisted in the return of contrabands to their owners. But he continued to deny "civilians," slaves included, admission to Union military camps and he ordered his officers not to allow slaves to follow troops on the march—the practice of General Lane in western Missouri.[67]

"If Slaves of Rebels, Free Them"

Without explicitly chastising Halleck, the president made it clear that he sided with Lane. "The Liberator" had arrived back in Washington in December and met with Lincoln on January 19, 1862, along with a small group of congressmen, senators, and other federal officials. Lane's activities as well as his unrepentant speeches endorsing the administration's policy of military emancipation were widely reported in the national press, and Lincoln was clearly aware of them when they met at the White House. Toward the end of the meeting, as Lane was preparing to return to Kansas, he addressed the president.

"Well, Mr. Lincoln," Lane said, "you know my way; I shall pursue the policy with which I began, and somebody will get hurt."

"Yes, General, I understand you," Lincoln replied. "And the only difference between you and me is, that *you* are willing to surrender fugitives to loyal owners in case they are willing to return; while *I do not believe the United States Government has any right to give them up in any case.* And if it had, the People would not permit us to exercise it."[68] Clearly, Lincoln's position was becoming more radical. Back in June of 1861 he was willing to allow the loyal owners from loyal states to recover fugitives on their own. But six months later, in the wake of strenuous criticism of Union officers who allowed loyal masters to reclaim their fugitives from army camps, Lincoln adopted the more radical position advocated by antislavery constitutionalists. Slaves who came within Union lines were on "free soil" and were, under the Constitution, presumptively free. The federal government had no right to return such persons to their putative owners; to do so would deprive them of their liberty without due process of law.

Democratic editors tried to discredit the report of Lincoln's exchange with Lane after it was published in the *New York Tribune* on January 21, 1862. But the reporter, W. A. Croffut, stood his ground, went back to his sources, and two days later confirmed that Lincoln had fully embraced the forfeiture-of-rights doctrine. "I am authorized by those who were present at the conversation at the White House between President Lincoln, Gen. Lane, and Senator Pomeroy, to assure you again that the idea which the President intended to assert, and did assert, was distinctly this:

> That the rebel States having, by their own insane action, abolished Slavery in all its relations with our Government by repudiating our protection, they can make no claim on us for fugitives, and that therefore the United States

cannot return them, either with the military or civil arm, without enslaving free men.[69]

Less than a week later Lincoln's cabinet explicitly instructed Lane to free slaves of rebel owners. "If slaves come within our lines from plantations beyond the federal lines, use them," Lane was told. "If they can work on fortifications use their services, clothe, feed and pay them. If absolutely necessary, arm them. *If slaves of rebels, free them.*" According to the report, this was "the administration programme, so far as Gen. Lane's expedition is concerned."[70]

The words and sentiments attributed to Lincoln were consistent with the warning he had issued back in Cincinnati in September 1859, a warning he reiterated in his inaugural address of March 4, 1860. If the slave states seceded from the Union they would forfeit the right of recaption secured by the Constitution, and the federal government would no longer be under any obligation to return fugitive slaves to their owners. In fact there was nothing in Lincoln's warning that was out of the ordinary among antislavery politicians. To be sure, the attack on Fort Sumter had altered the conditions under which the federal government dealt with "fugitives from service." Slaves escaping from disloyal states and owners had become "contraband of war," and as of August 8, 1861, they were emancipated. But the contraband policy, though novel, was nevertheless consistent with decades-old doctrine regarding military emancipation as well as the widely rehearsed claim that with secession the slaveholders would forfeit their constitutional right to recapture "fugitives from service."

More surprising was the rapidly radicalizing approach to fugitives of loyal owners from loyal slave states. The report of Lincoln's claim that the federal government could not return fugitive slaves even to loyal owners came at the same moment, January of 1862, as the administration's decision to release fugitive slaves held in the Blue Jug after thirty days. No doubt Lincoln was responding to the pressure coming from above and below, from Capitol Hill and from escaping slaves. House Republicans had made it clear as early as July 1861 that the army had no business enforcing the Fugitive Slave Act, and in March 1862 Congress revised the Articles of War to make it a crime for anyone in the military to participate in the capture and return of fugitive slaves. As Senator Cowan had pointed out, soldiers lacked the judicial authority to distinguish contrabands from fugitives and were prohibited from attempting to do so. That much was consistent with the well-established precepts of antislavery constitutionalism. But the revised Articles of War made no distinction between loyal masters from loyal states and disloyal masters from seceded states. Republicans in both Congress and the executive branch decreed that slaves escaping from loyal owners in loyal states could not, as a matter of policy, be returned to their owners by anyone in the Union army or navy. Even if the Republican Congress had averted its eyes, the number of slaves escaping from the loyal state of Maryland would have forced the issue. Clearly, the contingencies of war were pushing Union antislavery policy in an increasingly radical direction.

Yet as radical as the policy was, it was also the logical extension of one of the guiding principles of antislavery constitutionalism—the presumption of freedom to which

accused fugitives were entitled once they were no longer
under the legal authority of a slave state. Years—decades—
of northern resistance to fugitive slave catchers had condi-
tioned Lincoln and his fellow Republicans to assume from
the moment the war began that slaves would take advantage
of the arrival of invading Union armies to free themselves. A
correspondent for the *New York Tribune* traveling with Lane's
Kansas Brigade referred to the slaves who came within
Union lines as "self-freedmen," as though it was obvious to
his readers what that meant.[71] No one could have anticipated
the various contingencies thrown up by the war, but anyone
could have anticipated that when the war came Lincoln and
the Republicans would respond to its myriad eventualities in
ways that reflected their long-standing commitment to the
principles of antislavery constitutionalism.

The increasingly radical drift of Lincoln's policy culmi-
nated in the Emancipation Proclamation of January 1, 1861.
Technically, he continued to apply the loyalty test by decree-
ing the freedom of slaves in all the disloyal parts of the South
while exempting the loyal areas. But he abandoned any pre-
tense that the Union army would differentiate between loyal
and disloyal owners within rebellious areas. And even the
loyal areas of the South were not quite as exempt as they
seemed to be. For one thing, Union soldiers were now barred
by law from participating in the capture and return of fugitives, no matter where they were operating. Nor did the
Emancipation Proclamation exempt loyal areas from the
new policy of enlisting Black soldiers into the Union army.
There was no doubt about the radicalism of Lincoln's new
emancipation policy. The question was, would it work?

⟫⟫ 6 ⟪⟪

"A King's Cure"

Lincoln and the Origins of the Thirteenth Amendment

I N 1839, at the sixth annual meeting of the American Anti-
Slavery Society in New York City, the abolitionist Henry
Stanton proposed the following:

> Resolved, that the political power of the free States is suf-
> ficient, if properly exercised, to ultimately exterminate
> slavery in the nation.

Stanton then spoke at some length in favor of his resolution,
explaining in precise terms what the free states could do to
"ultimately exterminate" slavery. At the national level, Congress could ban slavery from the territories, abolish slavery in
the District of Columbia, prohibit the interstate slave trade,
and deny admission of any new slave states into the Union.
Acting on their own, the free states could establish the presumption of freedom so that "the moment a slave comes,
with the master's consent, within the bounds of the State, his

chains fall off, and he is *ipso facto* free." Northern states could also inhibit slave catchers from the South by guaranteeing alleged fugitives the rights of due process, such as habeas corpus and trial by jury. Stanton's list of policies was similar to the one enshrined in the Anti-Slavery Society's founding documents six years earlier. Congress could do all these things to undermine slavery, Stanton argued, but like most abolitionists—like most Americans—Stanton accepted that under the Constitution Congress had no power to abolish slavery directly in a state where it existed. However, by isolating the slave states and surrounding them with a "cordon of freedom," Congress and the northern legislatures could create the conditions that would compel the slave states to abolish slavery on their own.

But what if that didn't work, Stanton wondered. What if the South resisted all the pressure the federal government and the free states could bring to bear? In that case, the North had a "*dernier resort*," a last resort. "We will alter the constitution and bring slavery in the States within the range of Federal legislation," Stanton explained, "and then annihilate it at a blow." But wasn't that scenario "beyond the reach of possibility," Stanton asked. It takes three-fourths of the states to ratify a constitutional amendment, and at that moment there were too many slave states and not enough free states to make ratification even remotely feasible.

Stanton, however, conjured up a scenario whereby, in the not-so-distant future, it would be possible to abolish slavery "at a blow" by means of a constitutional amendment. "[I]f no new slave States are admitted to the Union," he argued, it will not be long before "three fourths of the confederacy will be undefiled with slavery." The key to this outcome was the Border States. "A close observer will discover from the signs of the times," Stanton predicted, "that many years will not have passed ere Kentucky, Virginia, Maryland, Delaware, and Missouri emancipate their slaves." With enough pressure, Florida might also abolish slavery—especially if the interstate slave trade were prohibited. Stanton then did the necessary calculations. There were at that moment—1839—thirteen free states in the Union. If six more free states were carved out of the northwestern territories, and six border slave states abolished slavery, "the twenty-five free States will rise as one man. . . . The Constitution will be altered, and slavery and its brother Lynch law, be hurled into their graves."[1]

In one sense, Stanton's prediction could scarcely have been more wrong. The trajectory of American history seemed to be moving in the opposite direction. Beginning in the late eighteenth century, a vast cotton kingdom arose, transforming the old South into the largest and wealthiest slave society on earth—maybe the largest in human history. Between 1789 and 1850 nine slave states and eight free states were admitted to the Union. The Mexican-American War ended with the acquisition of an immense southwestern territory that could potentially add several more slave states to the nation. Stanton's political agenda had also been severely constrained. In 1841 the Supreme Court ruled that Congress had no power to regulate the interstate slave trade, and antislavery activists thereafter abandoned most proposals to do so. In 1850 Congress passed a draconian fugitive slave law that *increased* federal power to capture escaped slaves in the free states. And having successfully beaten back a northern attempt to ban slavery from all of the Mexican cession, Congress in 1854 repealed the Missouri Compromise that had long banned slavery from the northwestern territories, once again increasing the likelihood of more slave states, rather than fewer. By 1860 not a single southern state had abolished slavery and the ratio of slave to free states made an abolition amendment all but inconceivable. The "ultimate extermination" of slavery seemed further removed from the realm of possibility than it was when Stanton calculated the odds a generation earlier.

But from the perspective of the slave states Stanton's forecast did not seem all that far-fetched. When they looked back on the nation's history, many southern leaders discerned a menacing shift in the balance of power between slave and free states. In 1776, when the American colonies declared their independence, the new nation included thirteen slave states and no free states. By 1850 things had changed dramatically. The number of slave states had increased slightly, from thirteen to fifteen, whereas the number of free states had leaped from zero to the same number, fifteen. This was the "equilibrium" to which John C. Calhoun referred in his famous last speech to the Senate on March 4, 1850. The dying South Carolinian proposed a series of constitutional amendments that would permanently equalize the power of the slave and free states in the federal government. It was an improbable proposal, but an influential argument.

Among northern congressmen and senators, the shift in the balance of power between slave and free states prompted two general observations. First, given the more rapid increase in northern population and the steady increase in the number of free states, why did the slave states continue to exercise such disproportionate clout in the federal government? Opponents of slavery answered that question by positing the existence of a "Slave Power" that operated, by various means, to dominate the presidency, the Supreme Court, and Congress.[2]

But northerners also argued that the Slave Power was doomed because the shift in the balance of power between slave and free states could not be stopped—whether because the northern economy was more dynamic, or because the North's population growth was rapidly outpacing the South's, or because slavery could not thrive in the arid Southwest and had nowhere left to expand. Whatever the reason, it was only a matter of time before the slave states were completely overshadowed—overwhelmed—by the rapid expansion in the number of free states.

In 1850 such predictions were iterated and reiterated, from one end of the northern political spectrum to the other. Senator Stephen Douglas of Illinois, a Democrat who was attentive to the interests of his southern colleagues, nevertheless warned that any attempt to maintain an "equilibrium" between slave and free states by artificially imposed legal means was bound to fail because climate and geography ensured that "liberty" would outpace "slavery" across the continent. At the same time William Seward, the radical antislavery senator from New York, claimed that the free labor economy of the North was so obviously superior to the slave economy of the South that no statutes or constitutional amendments could forestall the inevitable supremacy of the free states.

So when, in December 1849, President Zachary Taylor proposed the immediate admission of California as a free state, southerners in Congress—mostly from the cotton states—denounced it as a grave threat to slavery. The House of Representatives, they pointed out, was already dominated by northern states, despite the advantage that the three-fifths clause gave to the slave states. The equilibrium survived only in the Senate, where the votes of fifteen slave states could fend off any threats emanating from the fifteen free states. The nation was at a tipping point. The admission of California, and probably of New Mexico, as free states would forever upset the balance of power between the North and the South. And for that reason, a majority of southern congressmen spoke in opposition to Taylor's proposal.

Jefferson Davis, the senator from Mississippi and future president of the Confederacy, was one of the first to sound the southern alarm. On February 12, 1850, a few weeks after the president's California proposal was presented to Congress, Davis warned his fellow senators of what he called "the preponderating aggressive majority" in the North whose "cold, calculating purpose" was to "seek for sectional domination." This antislavery majority would achieve its political purpose by systematically violating the slaveholders' constitutional right to property in man. The interests of the North and the South were so clearly at odds, Davis explained, that "without a balance of power such as will enable every interest to protect itself—without such checks and restraints" on the "preponderating" majority, "the great purposes of this Union can never be preserved." Davis sincerely hoped to preserve the Union, but the "essential means" of doing so was to ensure that "in one branch of Congress the North and in the other the South should have a majority of representation." If all federal legislation were "restricted and balanced" in this way, "Congress would never be able to encroach upon the right and institutions of any portion of the Union." This could be accomplished by extending the Missouri Compromise line to the Pacific, thus dividing California into a free state north of the line and a slave state south of the line.[3]

Fail to maintain the equilibrium and the consequences would be dire, Davis warned. The number of free states would continue to grow, the increase in the number of slave states would be arrested, and at some point in the future the balance would become so lopsided that the free states would be able to rewrite the Constitution itself, abolishing slavery nationwide.

Davis's fear of a "preponderating" majority of northern states was the nightmarish inversion of the dream that abolitionist Henry Stanton had conjured up in 1839. The Antislavery Project, as Stanton outlined it, depended on the continued northward shift in the balance of sectional power. Admit only free states into the Union. Pressure the slave states to abolish slavery on their own, beginning with the Border States where slavery was weakest. The "ultimate extinction" of slavery would happen state by state, one state at a time, a prospect many southern leaders saw, reasonably enough, as a genuine threat to slavery.

Calhoun and his followers lost the battle over California. It was admitted to the Union as a free state in late 1850. There were now sixteen free states and fifteen slave states. Before the decade was out two more free states entered the Union—

Minnesota in 1858 and Oregon in 1859. A desperate effort by proslavery forces to bring Kansas into the Union as a slave state was thwarted by antislavery northerners. By the time Abraham Lincoln was elected president in November 1860 there were eighteen free states and still fifteen slave states—a balance of forces now sufficient to elect the first antislavery president with northern votes alone, but still hardly enough to rewrite the Constitution.

Rising to speak in the Georgia legislature on November 19, 1860, Henry Benning warned that "Mr. Lincoln's election to the Presidency is the abolition of slavery." How was this possible? "The North has now eighteen States, and the South fifteen," Benning noted. The political power that flowed from the preponderance of northern states, together with Lincoln's election, meant that "we shall have no more slave States from the public territory." Those 50,000 square miles were "sufficient to form twenty States. . . . Add to these the other eighteen, and you have thirty-eight. But this is not all," Benning went on. In the Border States of the South, slavery was either declining—as in Maryland, Kentucky, and Delaware—or stagnant, as in Virginia and Missouri. "In the process of time, and that no long time, these States will become free States." Eventually, Benning predicted, "slavery will be compressed into the eight cotton states. . . . When that time comes, and indeed long before that time come, the North—the Black Republican party (for that will be the North) will have it in its power only to amend the Constitution, and take what power it pleases upon the subject of slavery."[4] Benning may not have been a representative secessionist but his prediction was, more or less, accurate.

To be sure, Benning's support for secession as the best way to protect slavery turned out to be a spectacular miscalculation, but it was not a hysterical overreaction to a nonexistent threat. The shift in the balance of power on which Benning rested his prediction was real, and the threat it represented was real. The irony—the supreme irony—was that secession and war actually propelled that shift so that by 1865 the abolition amendment that Benning warned against became a reality. There had been no reasonable possibility of that happening on the day Lincoln was elected, and yet on the day he was assassinated the abolition amendment was well on the way to ratification. Historians sometimes tell us that the destruction of slavery was the incidental by-product of the war, that the war "changed everything." It would be more accurate to say that slavery was abolished because the Civil War radically *accelerated* the decades-long shift in the balance of power between slave and free states.

The acceleration began immediately as soon as the slave states seceded. In the space of about one month—between December 1860 and January 1861—six slave states withdrew from the Union, the last of them Louisiana, which seceded on January 26. Three days later, on January 29, Congress was finally able to admit Kansas to the Union as a free state. The departure of six slave states from Congress suddenly gave the antislavery forces a majority that enabled them to do what they had been unable to do ever since the passage of the Kansas-Nebraska Act in 1854. There were now nineteen free states and fifteen slave states. The subsequent secession of five more slave states handed the antislavery Republicans effective domination of both houses of Congress for the remainder of the war.

Combined with their control of the executive branch, Republicans would use their power to implement the Antislavery Project—a project substantially unchanged from its first iteration by Benjamin Lundy in 1821. The Lincoln administration quickly secured a treaty with Great Britain to suppress the Atlantic slave trade. The president himself ordered the first prosecution of an American sea captain to be convicted and hanged for trading slaves illegally. Whether by design or default, the Union naval blockade of the South shut down the coastwise slave trade. In addition, the federal government effectively stopped enforcing the Fugitive Slave Act. Congress abolished slavery in Washington, DC. It banned slavery from the western territories, in open defiance of the Supreme Court.

Not only were no slave states admitted to the Union, Congress actually required abolition as a condition for admission to the Union—something northern opponents of slavery had wanted to do ever since the Missouri Crisis in 1820. Within weeks of Virginia's secession, for example, mass meetings erupted in the western counties leading to the creation of an entirely separate state. But before West Virginia was allowed to enter the Union, the Republican Congress required the abolition of slavery as a condition for admission, and in 1863 West Virginia joined the Union as a free state. A year later, in October 1864, Nevada was admitted to the Union with abolition stipulated in its constitution. The count was now twenty-two free states to fifteen slave states.

But the steady admission of new free states would do nothing to diminish slavery in the fifteen states where it was legal. Even if the Republicans were thinking about a future abolition amendment—which they were not when the war began—it would have taken forty-five free states—sixty states in total—to ratify such an amendment. That would be impossible even today. But then, amending the Constitution was not a Republican goal at that time. The goal was to get the slave states to abolish slavery on their own, beginning with the four border slave states that did not secede—Delaware, Maryland, Kentucky, and Missouri. And this is where Abraham Lincoln gets really interesting.

Most often when we think about Lincoln's role in the destruction of slavery, we zero in on the Emancipation Proclamation. His fixation on the Border States in the first year of the war is widely interpreted as an obstacle to emancipation, a fixation Lincoln had to abandon before he could commit himself to the abolition of slavery. But what if putting pressure on the Border States *was* the abolitionist project?[5] In the 1830s, for example, the pioneering abolitionist James Gillespie Birney had argued that nationwide abolition would commence with abolition in Maryland, Virginia, and Kentucky. What if Lincoln never abandoned that project? What if the Emancipation Proclamation was part of the same project, now radicalized by the war? In truth, Lincoln's object all along was to get the slave states to abolish slavery on their own. He was always skeptical that emancipating individual slaves, even in large numbers, would ever be enough. Getting slavery abolished by emancipating slaves was not the goal, it was a means by which to achieve the goal. Lincoln was prepared to use whatever constitutional authority he had at his disposal to pressure the states to abolish slavery on their own. The Emancipation Proclamation turned out to be the most effective tool for exerting that pressure.

Lincoln's enduring commitment to state abolition is consistent with generations of antislavery agitation, but it does not square easily with the familiar story we've all been told of Lincoln's dramatic conversion from gradual abolition to immediate emancipation. That familiar story goes something like this:

In November 1861 Lincoln drafted two proposals for gradual, compensated abolition in Delaware, proposals he viewed as models for all the Border States to follow. Building on the abolition statutes passed by the northern states in the late eighteenth century, Lincoln suggested a gradual timetable for slavery's eventual abolition, along with federal compensation should Delaware—or any other slave state—adopt the proposal.[6] This was not the same as military emancipation. Indeed, by the time Lincoln drafted the Delaware proposals his administration was already implementing the First Confiscation Act, freeing all slaves—immediately and without compensation—who came within Union lines from disloyal states or disloyal masters. Emancipation of this sort was one of the war powers of the Constitution; freeing slaves was a military action. But Delaware was not at war with the Union and was technically beyond the reach of military emancipation. And because there were so few slaves in Delaware, Lincoln thought it was the best state to begin applying pressure to abolish slavery. Alas, the Democrats who controlled the Delaware legislature angrily rejected the proposals.

Undeterred, Lincoln went public on March 6, 1862, in a message to Congress urging it to "co-operate with any state which may adopt gradual abolishment of slavery, giving to such state pecuniary aid, to be used by such state in its discretion, to compensate for the inconveniences public and private, produced by such change of system."[7] Yet if Lincoln's proposal was consistent with long-standing abolitionist goals, the radicalizing impact of the Civil War was already evident in his March 6 address. Lincoln was offering direct federal compensation to states that passed gradual abolition statutes, a much more aggressive use of federal power than Birney and his followers had envisioned.

The radicalizing effect of the war was still more apparent in the way Lincoln began using the military conflict itself to encourage abolition by the Border States. Confederate leaders assumed that if they secured the South's independence, the four slave states that remained loyal to the Union would eventually secede and take their natural place in a slaveholding nation. Abolition by the Border States would deprive the Confederacy of that possibility, Lincoln believed, and "substantially ends the rebellion."[8] War had thereby added an element of urgent military necessity to the familiar abolitionist program of state-by-state abolition.

In still other ways Lincoln cited the war to justify a more aggressive approach to state abolition. Because waging war cost more than compensating states for abolishing slavery, for example, Lincoln calculated that his proposal would save the country money by hastening the end of the war. Finally, and most significantly, Lincoln issued ominous warnings to the effect that the longer the war went on the less likely it was that the Border States could be insulated from the subversive impact of military emancipation. "The incidents of the war can not be avoided," Lincoln explained in July 1862. "If the war continue long . . . the institution in your states will be extinguished by mere friction and abrasion—by the mere incidents of the war."[9] Lincoln was threating to use one policy—military emancipation—to force the states to adopt another, gradual abolition.

That threat was palpable because, despite the fact that military emancipation did not formally apply to the loyal slave states, the Republicans had adopted a number of policies that undermined slavery in those states without directly abolishing it. The First Confiscation Act had authorized the permanent forfeiture of slaves used in the rebellion, and the revised Articles of War made it a crime for anyone in the military to participate in the capture and return of fugitive slaves. Thereafter, as we've seen, when loyal masters from loyal states arrived at Union camps demanding the return of their slaves, they were told—or at any rate were supposed to be told—that they would have to find the fugitives on their own. Union troops—who had to pass through the Border States to get to the Confederacy—were a magnet for runaways, who quickly learned to secure the protection of federal officials by denouncing their owners as "secesh." By the middle of 1862 Border State representatives had to understand what Lincoln meant when he warned that, despite their loyalty to the Union, the "incidents of war" threatened to undermine slavery in their states. Nevertheless, they angrily rejected Lincoln's abolition proposal and denounced federal compensation as unconstitutional.

In standard accounts the harsh response of the Border States is said to have precipitated Lincoln's shift from gradual state abolition to immediate military emancipation. By the middle of 1862, the familiar story goes, the frustrated president at last gave up on gradual abolition by the loyal states and opted instead for the more radical policy of emancipation in the disloyal states. It took him a few months to announce his decision, but the announcement came on September 22, 1862, when Lincoln issued the Preliminary Emancipation Proclamation. In any area still in rebellion, Lincoln vowed, all the slaves would be emancipated one hundred days later on January 1, 1863, when he would issue the final proclamation. At that point the gloves would come off. No more compensation. No more gradualism. Lincoln even abandoned his long-standing commitment to colonization.

But then—halfway between the preliminary and final proclamations—came Lincoln's annual message to Congress on December 1, 1862, which has baffled historians ever since. Having vowed only weeks earlier to free all the slaves immediately and without compensation, Lincoln now reiterated his proposal for gradual, compensated state abolition, along with subsidies for the voluntary emigration of freed slaves. He aimed to overcome the objections of the Border States by repackaging his proposal in the form of a constitutional amendment that would allow Congress to compensate states and subsidize colonization. So what was Lincoln's policy, immediate emancipation or gradual abolition? Was Lincoln having second thoughts about issuing an emancipation proclamation?

Careful observers grasped that Lincoln's proposed

amendment would actually link state abolition to military emancipation so that the two policies worked hand in hand. They should be seen as "co-operative," the *Boston Journal* explained. The proclamation was a war measure that "dealt only with rebel communities" and involved "only the freeing of *individual* slaves." By comparison, Lincoln's proposed amendment was a legal rather than a military measure; it would apply to loyal areas operating "under the flag of the Union, so that the nineteenth century should close on no American slave." The problem with Lincoln's proposed constitutional amendment, at that point anyway, was that it would never be ratified. As Orestes Brownson pointed out, even if Republicans could muster two-thirds of the votes necessary to get Lincoln's amendment through both houses of Congress, it was highly unlikely to be ratified by three-fourths of the states. But Brownson was befuddled by Lincoln's proposal because, unlike the editors of the *Boston Journal*, he mistakenly believed that in issuing the Preliminary Emancipation Proclamation Lincoln had signaled a shift from gradual state-by-state abolition to immediate military emancipation.[10]

If Lincoln had made such a shift his December proposal would indeed be baffling. But if, instead, he viewed universal military emancipation as a powerful new inducement to state abolition—if the two policies had indeed become "co-operative"—his December speech poses no special problems. In fact, there was no shift from gradual state abolition to universal emancipation. Quite the contrary, the Emancipation Proclamation revived Lincoln's campaign for state abolition.

In mid-1863, six months after issuing the proclamation,

Lincoln began firing off a series of letters to civil and military officials—in the loyal states of Missouri and Maryland, but now also in the seceded states of Arkansas, Tennessee, Louisiana, even Florida—urging, nudging, pressuring, insisting—that their legislatures (now under loyal control) restore their states' normal relations with the Union by abolishing slavery on their own.

Lincoln's renewed campaign began with Missouri in late June 1863. The Union commander General John Schofield asked the president whether the federal government would protect the rights of slaveholders until the process of gradual abolition was complete. Lincoln was reluctant to pledge government support even for "temporary slavery," but he did not foresee any problems so long as Missouri's abolition program met two conditions—that it commenced immediately and was completed quickly. Gradual abolition was fine, Lincoln told Schofield, but "the period from the initiation to the final end, should be comparatively short."[11]

Disregarding Lincoln's advice, Missouri leaders endorsed a gradual abolition plan that would not begin for seven years. That, Lincoln complained, would leave too much time "to agitate for the repeal of the whole thing." Missouri's action forced Lincoln to stiffen, or at least clarify, his position on gradual abolition when he turned his attention to the state just south of Missouri. "It should begin at once," Lincoln wrote to General Stephen A. Hurlbut in Arkansas in late July 1863—one month after his letter to Schofield in Missouri. At the very least, Lincoln explained, any abolition law should give "the newborn, a vested interest in freedom, which could not be taken away." Now there were three requirements for state abolition: It still had to start right away, it still had to be completed quickly, but it also had to be irreversible. If the senator from Arkansas should propose such a plan—irrevocable abolition, to commence immediately and be completed quickly—"a single individual will have scarcely done the world so great a service," Lincoln said.[12]

He said almost the same thing a few weeks later to Andrew Johnson, then the military governor of Tennessee. After urging Johnson to set up a loyal state government as soon as possible, Lincoln noted that the governor had recently "declared in favor of emancipation in Tennessee, for which, may God bless you," Lincoln wrote. "Get emancipation into your new State government," he added, "and there will be no such word as fail in your case."[13]

However forceful Lincoln's language about abolition, he was not sure he had the legal authority to go beyond suggestions backed up by incentives. This was especially clear in the case of Louisiana, the state that most concerned the president in late 1863. In an early August letter to Union general Nathaniel Banks, Lincoln once again expressed his strong preference for abolition but also his reluctance to "direct" state affairs. "I very well know what I would be glad for Louisiana to do," he explained, but "it is quite another thing for me to assume direction of the matter." He hoped to see Louisiana "make a new Constitution recognizing the emancipation proclamation, and adopting emancipation in those parts of the state to which the proclamation does not apply."[14] Three months later, with no apparent progress, Lincoln wrote again to Banks, this time in a more exasperated tone. He was worried that there were loyal Louisianans who were prepared to set up a new state government while "repudiating the emancipation proclamation, and re-establishing slavery."[15]

Lincoln's sustained effort to get states to abolish slavery, *after* the Emancipation Proclamation had been issued, remains one of the least-understood features of his presidency. The confusion arises in part from the tendency to mistake the basic policy for the incentives Lincoln held out to the states to get them to adopt the policy. Compensation for the states that abolished slavery, subsidies for the voluntary colonization of free Blacks, a gradual timetable—those were not Lincoln's primary objectives. They were the means by which he hoped to achieve his objective—which was state abolition. So long as they seemed likely to push states toward abolition Lincoln continued to endorse those means. When they no longer suited his purpose, he abandoned them. After December 1862, for example, Lincoln never mentioned colonization again. By early 1864 he abandoned the gradual timetables as well.

Those incentives were no longer necessary, thanks to the intensified threat of military emancipation, a threat enhanced by the growing number of African Americans serving in the US army. Long before the Emancipation Proclamation, the Republicans had adopted policies that were undermining slavery in the Border States. The proclamation increased that pressure in two ways. Before Lincoln issued it, US soldiers were forbidden to entice slaves away from their farms and plantations. If slaves came into Union lines they were emancipated, but US soldiers were forbidden to recruit slaves. After January 1, 1863, the ban on enticement was lifted and the Union army began actively encouraging slaves to come within its lines.[16]

Second, and perhaps more importantly, the proclamation opened the Union military to the "armed" service of Black soldiers. A common criticism of the proclamation is that it exempted the loyal slave states—the very states where the US government was in a position to enforce its will. But the loyal slave states were not exempt from the provision opening the Union army to the enlistment of Black soldiers. On the contrary, in 1863 the War Department began aggressively recruiting slaves in Tennessee, Kentucky, Maryland, and Missouri—states supposedly exempt from the proclamation. Moreover, the government promised slave recruits freedom in return for military service, a promise that affected only the Border States.

The United States Colored Troops was created a few months after Lincoln's proclamation and went into operation in mid-1863, at the very same time Lincoln revved up the pressure on various states to abolish slavery altogether. Later in the year Lincoln endorsed Secretary of War Edwin M. Stanton's policy of enlisting slaves from the Border States against the will of their masters and in the face of intense protests from the governors of those states. As a result of Lincoln's policy, a disproportionate number of slaves who enlisted in the US army came from loyal parts of the South that were formally exempted from the emancipation provisions of Lincoln's proclamation. Here was "friction and abrasion" not as the incidental by-product of war, as Lincoln made it seem, but as deliberate policy.

Yet in the campaign Lincoln undertook in mid-1863 to

get various states to abolish slavery he always stopped short of requiring them to do so. He still believed that the federal government had "no lawful power" to abolish slavery in any state. In December 1863, however, Lincoln hit on an ingenious way to bypass this constitutional restriction. If he could not force a state to abolish slavery, perhaps he could require the citizens of disloyal states to endorse the Emancipation Proclamation. Lincoln announced the new policy in his "Proclamation of Amnesty and Reconstruction." Before they could vote or hold office, southern whites had to swear not only to preserve, protect, and defend the US Constitution, but also to "faithfully support all proclamations of the President made during the existing rebellion having reference to slaves."[17] For one brief period, lasting barely two months, Lincoln adopted the loyalty oath as an indirect means of getting formerly rebellious states to abolish slavery.

The most forceful attempt to implement the new policy was in Florida where, in January 1864, Lincoln learned of efforts "to reconstruct a loyal state government." He dispatched his personal secretary, John Hay, to assist in what turned out to be a futile effort to restore Florida to the Union. In the meantime the president wrote to Major General Quincy A. Gillmore instructing him not only to give the Florida restoration movement all the support he could but also to make it clear that former rebels returning to the Union had to swear the oath he had prescribed a month earlier in his amnesty proclamation. "I wish the thing done in the most speedy way possible," Lincoln wrote, but "when done," he added, it should "lie within the range of the late proclamation on the subject." Lincoln wanted the state back in the Union, but to get there Floridians would have to swear to "faithfully support" the Emancipation Proclamation.[18]

An oath to uphold the Emancipation Proclamation was yet another device to pressure states to act on their own, but it was a clumsy and inefficient way to get slavery abolished without actually violating the constitutional ban on direct federal abolition. By merely endorsing the Emancipation Proclamation, for example, slavery would still be legal in the states, even if all the slaves had been emancipated. Nor did the oath eliminate the lingering possibility of re-enslavement by the states after the war was over. At best the oath would forcibly link the Emancipation Proclamation to state abolition.

A few weeks after Lincoln announced his loyalty oath, however, Republicans in Congress came up with a better idea—a Thirteenth Amendment to the Constitution, by which three-quarters of the states would abolish slavery nationwide. That would solve all the problems associated with Lincoln's cumbersome loyalty oaths. An earlier "thirteenth amendment," the so-called Corwin amendment proposed during the secession crisis, would have preserved intact the existing federal consensus, which had always prevented Congress from abolishing slavery in a state—something Congress never did even during the Civil War, even without the Corwin amendment. The actual Thirteenth Amendment bypassed the states entirely, abolishing slavery nationwide upon ratification. But it had to be ratified by the states, and at that point—December of 1863—there were too many slave states and not enough free states to secure ratification. State-by-state abolition would have to continue. As a result the federal consensus, rather than an insuperable obstacle to abolition, was the method by which the Thirteenth Amendment was secured.

Still more paradoxical was the fact that the proposed amendment worked to inspire the states Lincoln was already pressuring to abolish slavery on their own. In January 1864, Arkansas Unionists petitioned the president to endorse their plan for a new state constitution that incorporated the language of the recently proposed Thirteenth Amendment. Lincoln quickly came around to supporting the new approach. He forwarded the Unionist petition to the military commander in Arkansas, Major General Frederick Steele, instructing him to "order an election immediately . . . according to the foregoing" petition. Fully aware that the Arkansas plan was different from his own proposal, Lincoln wrote back to Steele a week later telling him to work closely with the state's Unionists to "harmonize the two plans into one." Above all, Lincoln explained, "[b]e sure to retain the free State constitutional provision in some unquestionable form." A few days later, Lincoln wrote yet another letter to Steele, effectively withdrawing his own proposal and instead wholeheartedly endorsing the Arkansas plan. He instructed the general to cooperate with the state's Unionists. "They seem to be doing so well," Lincoln wrote, "that possibly the best you can do would be to help them on their own plan."[19]

Within weeks after Lincoln had proposed the oath to "faithfully support" the Emancipation Proclamation, Arkansas came up with a simpler, more straightforward way to get slavery abolished. The state constitutional convention, meeting in January, proposed a new charter declaring that "neither slavery nor involuntary servitude" shall exist in the state.

On March 4, 1864, the new constitution was ratified by referendum. With that, Arkansas became the first slave state to abolish slavery in sixty years, this time immediately and without compensation.[20]

The readiness with which Lincoln abandoned gradual abolition is another indication that ending slavery was always more important to him than ending it gradually—that gradualism, like compensation and colonization, was a means to the end, not the end itself. "[My] expressions of preference for *gradual* over *immediate* emancipation, are misunderstood," Lincoln explained. He had thought a gradual timetable would make states more likely to abolish slavery, but if "those who are better acquainted with the subject" preferred immediate emancipation, "most certainly I have no objection." Lincoln's basic "wish," he explained, "is that all who are for emancipation *in any form*, shall co-operate." So when Arkansas went on to adopt immediate abolition in early 1864, Lincoln had no trouble endorsing it.[21]

Within a year five more slave states followed Arkansas's lead. In March 1864, a convention meeting in Alexandria and representing the loyal portion of Virginia adopted a constitutional amendment declaring that "[s]lavery and involuntary servitude, except for crime, is hereby abolished and prohibited in the State forever."[22] In September eligible voters in Louisiana endorsed a new free state constitution. A few weeks later, in October, Maryland held a referendum on a proposed constitution declaring simply that "[h]ereafter, in this State, there shall be neither slavery nor involuntary servitude." The constitution narrowly lost in the initial count, but when the soldiers' votes came in from the field the free

state constitution of Maryland was safely ratified. Even without the familiar incentives of colonization, compensation, or
gradualism, the campaign for state abolition was suddenly
succeeding.[23]

In what turned out to be his last annual message to Congress, in December 1864, Lincoln reviewed the progress
of state-by-state abolition. Though the movement was still
"short of complete success," he said, "thousands of citizens"
in Arkansas and Louisiana "have organized loyal state governments with free constitutions." He pointed to movement
"in the same direction" in Missouri, Tennessee, and—rather
too hopefully—Kentucky. "But Maryland presents the example of complete success," he said. Thanks to its recent ratification of a free state constitution abolishing slavery, "Maryland
is secure to Liberty and Union for all the future."[24]

Missouri and Tennessee were not far behind. In the
November elections radicals who endorsed the Thirteenth
Amendment won control of both houses of the Missouri state
legislature and immediately called for a convention to meet
in early 1865. On January 11 the Missouri convention overwhelmingly endorsed immediate, unconditional abolition.
Meanwhile in Tennessee, Andrew Johnson had finally succeeded in gathering delegates to a constitutional convention
in Nashville where, on January 9, they proceeded to abolish
slavery in the state.

None of these states abolished slavery because Abraham
Lincoln told them to abolish slavery. Rather, Lincoln and
the Republicans in Congress had taken advantage of the
war to undermine slavery in those states, shifting the balance of power to favor those who opposed slavery and, as

often, opposed the long-standing domination of their states by the slaveholding class. Each state was different, but in all of them the agency of the slaves, the empowerment of the non-slaveholders, and federal policy came together to create conditions that made abolition possible.

As more and more states were abolishing slavery Lincoln and congressional Republicans turned their attention to getting the Thirteenth Amendment through Congress.[25] But it would be a mistake to conclude that this third policy—a constitutional amendment—displaced the two previously existing policies of military emancipation and state abolition. For just as Republicans used military emancipation to goad the states into abolishing slavery, so too was state-by-state abolition the precondition for the success of the Thirteenth Amendment. In fact, all three antislavery policies, though theoretically distinct, actually worked in concert so that by January 1865 enough states had abolished slavery to make ratification of a nationwide abolition amendment possible.[26]

The policies Lincoln and the Republicans adopted had radically accelerated the shift in the balance of power between slave and free states, a shift that had begun long before in the 1780s when the first states began to abolish slavery on their own. The thirteen slave states of 1776 had become, by 1860, eighteen free and fifteen slave states. During the Civil War Republicans admitted three new free states to the Union—Kansas, West Virginia, and Nevada. More important, however, was the revolutionary impact that universal military emancipation and Black enlistment had on Lincoln's sustained campaign for state-by-state abolition. In the last year of the war, six slave states—Arkansas, Virginia,

Maryland, Missouri, Louisiana, and Tennessee—abolished slavery on their own—though under enormous pressure from the federal government to do so. To be sure, some of these "states" were barely even states. Virginia's legislature was entirely a creature of the federal government and at best claimed sovereignty over a handful of counties in proximity to Washington, DC. Louisiana's legislature was scarcely more representative of the state. Tennessee's even less so. But as far as the Lincoln administration was concerned, the only legitimate state government was a loyal state government, and in the president's accounting six "loyal" slave states had abolished slavery.

By the end of January 1865, at the moment Congress sent the Thirteenth Amendment out for ratification, the 1860 ratio of eighteen free states to fifteen slave states was long gone. By the US government's accounting there were now twenty-seven free states and nine slave states, the three-quarters proportion necessary for ratification. The campaign for state abolition had made the Thirteenth Amendment—inconceivable in 1860—feasible in 1865.

Precisely how feasible became clear shortly after February 1, the day Congress sent the amendment to the states for ratification. West Virginia, the first state ever required to abolish slavery as a condition for admission to the Union, ratified the amendment on February 3. The two free states admitted to the Union since Lincoln's election in 1860—Kansas and Nevada—ratified the amendment on February 7 and February 16, respectively. Then there were the votes of the states that had abolished slavery in the last year of the war. The Maryland House of Delegates was first off the mark, ratifying on February 1, the same day Congress endorsed the joint resolution. The Maryland state senate approved it two days later. By a joint resolution of its own two houses, the Missouri legislature ratified the amendment on February 10. Within a week both houses of the Louisiana legislature did the same. Next came Tennessee's state senate, on April 5, followed by its house of representatives two days later. Finally, Arkansas—the first slave state to abolish slavery on its own in more than half a century—ratified the Thirteenth Amendment on April 20, 1865.[27] By contrast, not one of the nine remaining slave states ratified the amendment until they were all but forced to do so by President Andrew Johnson in late 1865.

It's always dangerous to speculate about what might have been, but in this case it's safe to say that the six states that had abolished slavery, each of which quickly ratified the Thirteenth Amendment in the early months of 1865, would not have done so five years earlier. Radicalized by war, the long-standing Antislavery Project of using federal pressure to get the states to abolish slavery on their own made it possible to do what military emancipation alone could not—the complete and irreversible abolition of slavery everywhere in the United States. To the very end the states were the key. The irony—one that Henry Stanton suggested decades before— was that the culmination of antislavery constitutionalism was a major revision of the Constitution.

On February 1, 1865, the same day the House and Senate passed the joint resolution submitting the Thirteenth Amendment to the states for ratification, President Abraham Lincoln spoke briefly to a group of serenaders gathered out-

side the White House. He "supposed" that they had come to
celebrate. More than a year after it had been introduced, and
after months of grueling political struggle against a determined Democratic minority, the Republicans had at last succeeded in mustering the two-thirds vote they needed to get
an amendment abolishing slavery nationwide through the
House of Representatives. The amendment was necessary,
Lincoln explained, because his own Emancipation Proclamation of two years earlier was not enough to ensure the
destruction of slavery. As it was based on self-emancipation,
the proclamation applied only to "those who came into our
lines" and was "inoperative as to those who did not give
themselves up." Without the constitutional amendment millions of African Americans could remain enslaved, and their
children would be enslaved as well. Although he didn't mention it on this occasion, Lincoln had for years expressed the
added concern that when the Union was restored, the southern states would attempt to re-enslave those freed by means
of military emancipation during the war. "This amendment
is a King's cure for all the evils," Lincoln told the serenaders. "It winds the whole thing up." It would free all those still
enslaved when the Civil War ended. It would free their children. And it would preclude the possibility of re-enslavement.
It was hardly surprising, then, that Lincoln considered the
amendment "a great moral victory." But the victory was still
incomplete, Lincoln added; "there is a task yet before us."
The amendment still had to be ratified and that, he pointed
out, could only be done "by the votes of the States."[28]

Acknowledgments

LIKE EMANCIPATION, this book was in some ways bound to happen, in some ways serendipitous, and the outcome was not at all clear until very late in the day. I never planned to do a book about Lincoln, but my editor, Steve Forman, read an essay of mine on the origins of the Thirteenth Amendment and suggested I expand it into a short book. At about the same time, my friend Maeva Marcus had invited me to teach a seminar on antislavery constitutionalism. Joe Murphy and I compiled a series of documents for the course and we co-taught it at the George Washington University Law School. I taught it again at the New-York Historical Society, this time with Sean Wilentz. Conducting those seminars, alongside two superb historians, transformed how I think about slavery and the Constitution in ways I could never have imagined. So when Steve suggested the book, the light bulb went off and the struggle to put it all together commenced. If there's something worthwhile in the result, it's largely thanks to Steve, Maeva, Sean, and Joe.

Let me also thank a number of friends and colleagues who read and commented on the manuscript, saving me from errors and forcing me to clarify otherwise obscure points. Not all of them agree with my interpretation, which in some cases is precisely why I solicited their advice. Thanks, then, to Randy Barnett, Michael Burlingame, Greg Downs, Eric Foner, Don Herzog, Annette Gordon-Reed, Matt Karp, Jim McPherson, Matt Pinsker, David Waldstreicher, and Sean Wilentz. A long conversation with Akhil Amar made me especially aware of the difference between the way legal scholars and historians might approach the same subject. This is, emphatically, a historian's book.

In my younger days I was skeptical of all those authors' acknowledgments of students from whom they learned so much. Not anymore. Paul Polgar, John Blanton, and Joe Murphy have been roaming these intellectual fields for many years and have managed to impart to me a fraction of what they know about the legal history of slavery and antislavery. Thanks also to Evan Turiano, for sharing his rapidly expanding knowledge of the legal and political history of fugitive slaves, and to Graham Peck, a Lincoln scholar in his own right, for saving me from several errors, big and small. I imposed an early draft of the manuscript on Scott Ackerman, David Campmier, Edward Charnley, Mike Crowder, Jack Devine, Jaja Duangkamol, and Sean Griffin, and am grateful for their comments. And to all my students at the Graduate Center and Northwestern, many, many thanks—for enlightening me, correcting me, and arguing with me, and for making teaching so much fun.

I submitted what is now chapter five to the *Journal of the Civil War Era*. The editors of the journal asked me to add a good deal of historiography, but the editor of the book wanted historiography kept to a bare minimum. Contract law prevailed, I was obliged to do the book, and in the rush to completion the article fell by the wayside. But the journal's readers forced me to rethink the way I shaped the chapter, and I thank them for that.

Notes

Abbreviations

CW Roy Basler, ed., *Collected Works of Abraham Lincoln* (New Brunswick, NJ: Rutgers University Press, 1953)

ALP-LC Abraham Lincoln Papers, Manuscript Division, Library of Congress

OR *The War of the Rebellion: A Compilation of the Official Records of the War of the Union and Confederate Armies* (Washington, DC: Government Printing Office, 1880–1901)

Preface

1. *CW*, 4: 238–39. The allusion is to Psalm 137: "If I forget thee, O Jerusalem, let my right hand forget her cunning. If I do not remember thee, let my tongue cleave to the roof of my mouth."
2. *CW*, 4: 240.
3. *CW*, 2: 492.
4. On this point, see Jack N. Rakove, *Original Meanings: Politics and Ideas in the Making of the Constitution* (New York, 1996).
5. The pioneering historian of the origins of the Constitution's compromises with slavery is Staughton Lynd, "The Compromise of 1787," *Political Science Quarterly* 81, no. 2 (1966): 225–50. Paul

Finkelman, "Making a Covenant with Death: Slavery and the Constitutional Convention," in Richard Beeman, et al., eds., *Beyond Confederation: Origins of the Constitution and American National Identity* (Chapel Hill, 1987), pp. 188–225, is sharply critical of the compromises. Like Finkelman, George William Van Cleve, *A Slaveholders' Union: Slavery, Politics, and the Constitution in the Early American Republic* (Chicago, 2010), emphasizes the proslavery compromises. David Waldstreicher, *Slavery's Constitution: From Revolution to Ratification* (New York, 2009), demonstrates the pervasiveness of the problem of slavery, sees slavery and antislavery intimately intertwined but with the proslavery elements prevailing. Earl M. Maltz, "The Idea of a Proslavery Constitution," *Journal of the Early Republic* 17 (1997): 37–59 is critical of the proslavery interpretation.

Another group of scholars discern both proslavery and antislavery elements in the Constitution. See Donald Robinson, *Slavery in the Structure of American Politics, 1765–1820* (New York, 1971), pp. 168–247, esp. 243ff. Sean Wilentz, *No Property in Man: Slavery and Antislavery at the Nation's Founding* (Cambridge, MA, 2018), likewise sees proslavery and antislavery forces battling with each other, but is the first to highlight the critical refusal of the founders to protect slavery as a right of property. Don E. Fehrenbacher, *The Slaveholding Republic: An Account of the United States Government's Relations to Slavery*, completed and edited by Ward M. McAfee (New York, 2001), argues that the Constitution was formally neutral on slavery but that southern political domination led to the prevalence of a proslavery interpretation.

Astonishingly, there is no history of antislavery constitutionalism other than the groundbreaking study of William M. Wiecek, *The Sources of Antislavery Constitutionalism, 1790–1848* (Ithaca, 1977). Wiecek carries the story up to 1848, just as antislavery constitutionalism was entering the political mainstream. Legal scholars have been more attentive to the significance of antislavery constitutionalism, though chiefly for purposes of understanding the origins of Reconstruction. See especially Jacobus tenBroek, *Equal Under Law* (New York, 1965), originally published as *The Antislavery Origins of the Fourteenth Amendment* (Berkeley, 1951). More recently, Randy E. Barnett has expanded on tenBroek's argument in a number of thoroughly documented articles, perhaps most notably "Whence Comes Section One? The Abolitionist Origins of the Fourteenth Amendment," *Journal of Legal Analysis* 3, no. 1 (Spring 2011): 165–263.

6. It might also be that the cynical "antipolitics" of recent decades has made it difficult to grasp the broad political engagement of Americans in the constitutional issues of the Civil War era. For a recent example of how contemporary political cynicism is improbably imposed on an age when politics was a form of popular culture and voter turnout reached record numbers, see Daniel Crofts, *Lincoln and the Politics of Slavery: The Other Thirteenth Amendment and the Struggle to Save the Union* (Chapel Hill, 2016). On antebellum politics as a form of popular culture, see William E. Gienapp, "'Politics Seem to Enter into Everything': Political Culture in the North," in Stephen E. Maizlish and John J. Kushma, eds., *Essays on American Antebellum Politics, 1840–1860* (College Station, 1982), pp. 15–69. For a critique of the pervasive impact of antipolitical sentiment on recent scholarship in American history, see Sean Wilentz, *The Politicians and the Egalitarians: The Hidden History of American Politics* (New York, 2016).

1. "That Glorious Fabric of Collected Wisdom"

1. Herbert Aptheker, *A Documentary History of the Negro People in the United States*, vol. 1 (New York, 1951), p. 60.
2. *Freedom's Journal*, March 16, 1827.
3. *Congressional Globe*, July 22, 1848, p. 988.
4. *Speech of Hon. Charles Sumner, of Massachusetts, on his Motion to Repeal the Fugitive Slave Bill, in the Senate of the United States, August 26, 1852* (Boston, 1852), p. 29.
5. *CW*, 3: 543.
6. Michael Holt argues that party platforms were "all-important in 1860" and that they were "central to the story of that election." Michael F. Holt, *The Election of 1860: "A Campaign Fraught with Consequences"* (Lawrence, KS, 2017), p. xii.
7. David Brion Davis, *The Problem of Slavery in Western Culture; The Problem of Slavery in the Age of Revolution, 1770–1823* (Ithaca, 1975).

There remains substantial disagreement over what caused the remarkable shift, but most scholars agree that the origins of antislavery were somehow linked to the development of capitalism. See Thomas Bender, ed., *The Antilavery Debate: Capitalism and Abolitionism as a Problem in Historical Interpretation* (Berkeley and Los Angeles, 1992).

8. For the influence of slavery on the broader history of taxation, see Robin L. Eihnorn, *American Taxation, American Slavery* (Chicago, 2006).

9. William Blackstone, *Commentaries on the Laws of England*, 7th ed. (Oxford, 1775) 3: 4–5. "Recaption or *reprisal* is another species of remedy by the mere act of the party injured. This happens, when any one hath deprived another of his property in goods or chattels personal, or wrongfully detains one's wife, child, or servant: in which case the owner of the goods, the husband, parent, or master, may lawfully claim an retake them, wherever he happens to find them; so it be not in a riotous manner, or attended with a breach of peace."

10. On the intrinsic ambiguity of the fugitive slave clause, see H. Robert Baker, "The Fugitive Slave Clause and the Antebellum Constitution." *Law and History Review* 30, no. 4 (2012): 1133–74; Matthew Pinsker, "After 1850: Reassessing the Impact of the Fugitive Slave Law," in Damian Alan Pargas, Stanley Harrold, and Randall Miller, eds., *Fugitive Slaves and Spaces of Freedom in North America* (Gainesville, FL, 2018), pp. 95–96. The fugitive slave clause was located in Article IV of the Constitution, which regulates relations among states and between the states and the federal government. Implicitly, this meant that the clause recognized the role of the states in establishing legal processes for fugitive slave renditions. Over the ensuing decades the free states would pass dozens of "personal liberty" laws based on that constitutional premise. The standard history of personal liberty laws is Thomas D. Morris, *Free Men All: The Personal Liberty Laws of the North, 1780–1861* (Baltimore, 1974). For the text of the 1788 Pennsylvania statute, see http://www.ushistory .org/presidentshouse/history/amendment1788.php

11. The Confederation Congress passed the Northwest Ordinance, which banned slavery from US territory north of the Ohio River,

while the constitutional convention was meeting in New York. The ordinance was immediately reenacted by the first Congress meeting under the newly ratified Constitution. Proslavery settlers in the territory sometimes petitioned to have the ban on slavery lifted on the grounds that it was unconstitutional, but Congress repeatedly rebuffed them. Well into the first decade of the nineteenth century southern congressmen agreed that the Constitution gave Congress the power to ban slavery in the territories.

12. Lincoln once said that by not using the word "slave" in the Constitution the founders hid it away like a disfiguring disease, but his point was not that the founders were embarrassed by what they had done but that slavery itself was shameful.

13. Paul J. Polgar, *Standard-Bearers of Equality: America's First Abolition Movement* (Chapel Hill, 2019), documents both the breadth and depth of antislavery sentiment in the middle states during and after the American Revolution.

14. Quotations in Wilentz, *No Property in Man*, 94ff.

15. Kaminski, John P., ed., *A Necessary Evil? Slavery and the Debate over the Constitution* (Lanham, MD). In the nearly one hundred pages of documents Kaminsky reprints, there is a single reference to the fugitive slave clause in a private letter. There appears to have been no public debate on it.

16. Kaminski, ed., *A Necessary Evil?* p. 89.

17. Bailyn, Bernard, ed., *Debate on the Constitution, Part One* (Princeton, 1955), p. 830.

18. Bailyn, ed., *Debate on the Constitution, Part One*, pp. 931–92.

19. Wilentz, *No Property in Man*, p. 130.

20. Kaminski, ed., *A Necessary Evil?* p. 121.

21. Wiecek, *Sources of Antislavery Constitutionalism*; James Oakes, *Freedom National: The Destruction of Slavery in the United States* (New York, 2013).

22. Bailyn, ed., *Debate on the Constitution, Part One*, p. 915.

23. On the widespread acceptance of the federal consensus, see Daniel Crofts, *Lincoln and the Politics of Slavery: The Other Thirteenth Amendment and the Struggle to Save the Union* (Chapel Hill, 2016).

24. *The Declaration of Sentiments and Constitution of the American Anti-Slavery Society* (New York, 1835).

25. *CW*, 4: 250.

26. Bailyn, ed., *Debate on the Constitution, Part Two*, 454.

27. House report on the "Abolition of Slavery," 1st Cong., 2nd Sess., Doc. 13.

28. *Observations of Rufus King, on the Missouri Bill* (Philadelphia, 1819). Emphasis added.

29. Joshua Giddings, *Pacificus: The Rights and Privileges of the Several States in Regard to Slavery* (1842).

30. *Congressional Globe*, May 21, 1844 (appendix), p. 706.

31. Arthur M. Schlesinger Jr., and Fred L. Israel, eds., *History of American Presidential Elections*, vol. 1 (New York, 1971), p. 801.

32. Jonathan Gienapp, *The Second Creation: Fixing the American Constitution in the Founding Era* (Cambridge, MA, 2018). Some would say that the meaning of the various clauses antagonists invoked really was "fixed" but that what was at stake was the overall implications of the mix of pro- and antislavery clauses.

33. The standard study of these anti-sojourn laws is Paul Finkelman, *An Imperfect Union: Slavery, Federalism, and Comity* (Chapel Hill, 1981).

34. On the willingness of many Republicans to advocate violations of the law, see Matthew Karp, "The People's Revolution of 1856: Antislavery Populism, National Politics, and the Emergence of the Republican Party," *Journal of the Civil War Era* 9, no. 4 (December 2019): 524–45.

35. *Gales and Seaton's History of Debates in Congress*, February 11, 1790, pp. 1225, 1231; House Report on the "Abolition of Slavery," 1st Cong., 2nd Sess., Doc. 13.

2. "Freedom Is the Rule, Slavery Is the Exception"

1. *Chicago Press and Tribune*, October 18, 1860.

2. *CW*, 2: 282.

3. *CW*, 4: 67. See also *CW*, 3: 512.

4. *Annals of Congress*, February 16, 1819, pp. 1207–8. On the antislavery demand for a complete ban on slavery in all the territory west of the Mississippi, see John Craig Hammond, "President, Planter, Politician: James Monroe, the Missouri Compromise, and the Politics of Slavery," *Journal of American History* 105 (March 2019): 843–67.

5. Curiously, no antislavery politician that I know of argued that the guarantee clause overrode the federal consensus and allowed Congress to abolish slavery in a state. It merely empowered Congress to require abolition as a condition for admission of a territory into the Union.

6. *Observations of Rufus King, On the Missouri Bill* (Philadelphia, 1819); *Annals of Congress,* January 27, 1820, pp. 952, 962.

7. James Oakes, *The Scorpion's Sting: Antislavery and the Coming of the Civil War* (New York, 2014), pp. 91–94.

8. *House Journal,* May 13, 1826, p. 560.

9. *Register of Debates,* January 6, 1829, p. 167.

10. *Register of Debates,* January 7, 1829, p. 175.

11. Quotations in Kate Masur, *Equal Before the Law: Race, Politics, and the Making of an American Promise* (New York, forthcoming), Chapter 4: "The Rights of the Citizens of Massachusetts." My thanks to Professor Masur for permission to cite her superb manuscript.

12. Aptheker, *A Documentary History of the Negro People in the United States,* p. 221, quoted from *The Liberator,* November 4, 1842.

13. Polgar, *Standard-Bearers of Equality.*

14. *Register of Debates,* March 1, 1836, p. 665.

15. *James G. Birney v. The State of Ohio.* 8 Ohio 230; 1837 Ohio Lexus 83.

16. Theodore Dwight Weld, *The Power of Congress over the District of Columbia* (New York, 1838).

17. William Jay, *View of the Actions of the Federal Government with Regard to Slavery* (New York, 1839). The forfeiture-of-rights doctrine had a major influence on the earliest federal moves against slavery during the Civil War, a subject taken up in Chapter 4.

18. Aptheker, *A Documentary History of the Negro People in the United States,* p. 130.

19. Aptheker, *A Documentary History of the Negro People in the United States,* p. 162.

20. Aptheker, *A Documentary History of the Negro People in the United States,* p. 165.

21. Aptheker, *A Documentary History of the Negro People in the United States,* p. 185.

22. *The Declaration of Sentiments and Constitution of the American Anti-Slavery Society* (New York, 1835).

23. Debates over the Jay Treaty (1794) reveal a virtual consensus on the right to emancipation in wartime, and the Treaty of Ghent (1814) expressly acknowledged the right, as had the Treaty of Paris (1783) even before the Constitution was established.

24. Oakes, *Scorpion's Sting*, pp. 104–65. The war powers clause would live on to become the primary justification for emancipation during the Civil War. See below, chapter 4.

25. William Lloyd Garrison to Rev. Samuel J. May, July 17, 1845, in Walter M. Merrill, ed. *The Letters of William Lloyd Garrison, vol. 3* (Cambridge, MA, 1973), p. 303.

26. Barnett, "Whence Comes Section One?" ably summarizes the thought of the major advocates of the view that the Constitution was so fundamentally antislavery that Congress *could* abolish slavery in a state. I call this "abolitionist constitutionalism," as distinguished from "antislavery constitutionalism," following the terminology of Manisha Sinha, *The Slave's Cause: A History of Abolition* (New Haven, 2016).

27. *The Liberator*, May 6, 1842.

28. Wendell Phillips, *The Constitution: A Pro-Slavery Compact* (New York, 1844). The same intellectual slippage between what the Constitution said and how proslavery politicians and their allies interpreted it reappears in Wendell Phillips, *Review of Lysander Spooner's Essay on the Unconstitutionality of Slavery* (Boston, 1847).

29. This is essentially the distinction adopted by Fehrenbacher, *The Slaveholders' Republic*.

30. William Goodell, *Views of American Constitutional Law: In its Bearing Upon American Slavery* (Utica, NY, 1944).

31. *Minutes of the State Convention, of the Colored Citizens of Ohio . . .* (Columbus, 1851), pp. 6–7, 8, 10.

32. By the 1850s Garrison's position had rendered him marginal to the larger antislavery movement, and abolitionist constitutionalists conceded that their own views had attracted few adherents. For an insightful study of the larger antislavery movement, see Bruce Laurie, *Beyond Garrison: Antislavery and Social Reform* (Cambridge, UK, 2005).

33. Joseph Murphy, "Neither a Slave Nor a King: The Antislavery Project and the Origins of the American Sectional Crisis, 1820–1848"

(PhD dissertation, Graduate Center of the City University of New York, 2016).

34. *Congressional Globe,* April 15, 1840, pp. 233, 329. On the shifting Atlantic legal context, see Joseph T. Murphy, "The British Example: West Indian Emancipation, the Freedom Principle, and the Rise of Antislavery Politics in the United States, 1833–1843," *Journal of the Civil War Era* 8, no. 4 (December 2018)" 621–46; Jeffrey R. Kerr-Ritchie, *Rebellious Passage: The* Creole *Revolt and America's Coastal Slave Trade* (Cambridge, UK, 2019).

35. *Congressional Globe,* March 21, 1842, p. 342.

36. See *Congressional Globe,* July 26, 1848, p. 1002, where Connecticut Senator Roger Baldwin proposes a due process suit by a slave as an amendment to Clayton's territorial bill.

37. *National Era,* September 23, 1847.

38. Arthur M. Schlesinger Jr., ed., *History of American Presidential Elections, 1789–1968,* vol. 2 (New York, 1971), pp. 902–5.

39. William Ellery Channing, *The Duty of the Free States; or, Remarks on the Creole Case* (Glasgow, 1842).

40. *Speech of William H. Seward on the Admission of California, delivered in the Senate of the United States, March 11, 1850* (Washington, 1850).

41. *Congressional Globe,* March 27, 1850, p. 477.

42. Aptheker, *A Documentary History of the Negro People in the United States,* pp. 424, 430.

43. *Proceedings of a Convention of the Colored Men of Ohio* (Cincinnati, 1858), pp. 15–16.

44. Eric Foner, *The Second Founding: How the Civil War and Reconstruction Remade the Constitution* (New York, 2019).

45. On African American claims of citizenship rights, see Andrew K. Diemer, *The Politics of Black Citizenship: Free African Americans in the Mid-Atlantic Borderland, 1817–1863* (Athens, GA, 2016); Martha Jones, *Birthright Citizens: A History of Race and Rights in Antebellum America* (New York, 2018).

46. *Minutes and Address of the State Convention of the Colored Citizens of Ohio* (Oberlin, 1849), pp. 21–25.

47. Aptheker, *A Documentary History of the Negro People in the United States,* p. 215. Quoted from *The Liberator,* February 25, 1842.

48. Aptheker, *A Documentary History of the Negro People in the United States*, p. 359, quoted from *The Liberator*, August 5, 1853.

49. *Proceedings of the State Convention of Colored Men, Held in the City of Columbus, Ohio, Jan. 16th, 17th & 18th, 1856* (Columbus, 1856?), p. 5.

50. The best account of the origins of birthright citizenship remains James H. Kettner, *The Development of American Citizenship, 1608–1870* (Chapel Hill, 1978); Rogers M. Smith, *Civic Ideals: Conflicting Visions of Citizenship in U.S. History* (New Haven, 1997), documents various efforts to restrict citizenship. See also Kunal M. Parker, *Making Foreigners: Immigration and Citizenship Law in America, 1600–2000* (New York, 2015).

51. The essay was one part of William Yates, *Rights of Colored Men: Suffrage, Citizenship, and Trial by Jury* (1838).

52. Giddings, *Pacificus*, essay I.

53. *Congressional Globe*, April 3, 1850, p. 422.

54. *"Freedom National; Slavery Sectional. Speech of Hon. Charles Sumner, of Massachusetts, On His Motion to Repeal the Fugitive Slave Bill* (Washington, 1853).

55. Aptheker, *A Documentary History of the Negro People in the United States*, p. 60.

56. *Annals of Congress*, January 1820, p. 958.

57. *Minutes and Proceedings of the First Annual Convention of the People of Colour, Held by Adjournments in the City of Philadelphia, From the Sixth to the Eleventh of June, inclusive, 1831* (Philadelphia, 1831), pp. 4–5.

58. *Minutes of the State Convention of Colored Citizens, held at Albany . . . For the Purpose of Considering their Political Condition* (New York, 1840), pp. 32–34.

59. *Minutes of the States Convention, of the Colored Citizens of the State of Michigan, Held in the City of Detroit on the 26th & 27th of October, 1843 . . .* (Detroit?, 1843?). Note that the online transcript [here:https:// docs.google.com/viewerng/viewer?url=http://coloredconventions .org/files/original/36d2c17138b0bf5fb35567df9b5208d8.pdf] does not contain the place and date of publication.

60. *Proceedings of the Colored National Convention, Held in Rochester, July 6th, 7th and 8th, 1853* (Rochester, 1853), p. 8.

61. *Congressional Globe*, February 15, 1850, p. 220.

62. *Speech of Mr. Horace Mann, of Mass., on the subject of slavery in the territories . . .* (Washington, 1850), p. 7.

63. Quoted in Francis Preston Blair, *A Voice from the Grave of Jackson! Letter from Francis P. Blair, Esq. to a public meeting in New York, held April 29, 1856* (Washington, 1856), p. 11.

64. *Speech of Hon. E.D. Baker, of Oregon: Delivered in the Senate of the United States, January 2d, and 3d, 1861, upon the secession question* (Washington City, 1861), p. 26.

65. Salmon P. Chase called slave ownership a "naked legal right." *Speech of Salmon P. Chase, in the Case of the Colored Woman, Matilda* (Cincinnati, 1837).

66. *Congressional Globe*, March 11, 1850 (appendix), pp. 264–65.

67. *Address of the Southern and Western Liberty Convention held at Cincinnati, June 11 and 12, 1845* (Cincinnati, 1845).

3. The Antislavery Project

1. On the Decatur convention as the origins of the Illinois Republican Party, see Don E. Fehrenbacher, *Prelude to Greatness: Lincoln in the 1850s* (Stanford, 1962: McGraw-Hill paperback ed., 1964), p 44; William E. Gienapp, *The Origins of the Republican Party, 1852–1856* (New York, 1987), pp. 288–89; Michael Burlingame, *Abraham Lincoln: A Life*, vol. 1 (Baltimore, 2008), pp. 411–15.

2. Lincoln had read the report of the Quincy convention, including the resolutions, in the *Quincy Whig*, August 4, 1855. A week later, in a letter to Owen Lovejoy, Lincoln indicated that he had no objection to joining a party based on the principles espoused at Quincy. "I lately saw, in the Quincy Whig, the report of a Preamble and resolutions" of the convention and, though he did not have them at hand, "so far as I can remember them, they occupy the ground I should be willing to 'fuse' upon." *CW*, 2: 316–17.

3. *Chicago Daily Tribune*, February 25, 1856.

4. *Illinois Chronicle*, February 28, 1856.

5. John L. Brooke, *"There is a North": Fugitive Slaves, Political Crisis, and Cultural Transformation in the Coming of the Civil War* (Amherst, 2019).

6. Every biography of Lincoln covers the Peoria address, but for

extended analyses, see Ronald C. White Jr., *The Eloquent President: A Portrait Through His Words* (New York, 2006); Burlingame, *Abraham Lincoln: A Life*, 1: 376–90; Lewis E. Lehrman, *Lincoln at Peoria: The Turning Point* (Mechanicsburg, PA, 2008).

7. *CW*, 2: 255.

8. *CW*, 2: 256.

9. *CW*, 2: 256.

10. Benjamin Lundy, *Genius of Universal Emancipation* (1821).

11. *The Declaration of Sentiments and Constitution of the American Anti-Slavery Society* (New York, 1835).

12. Stanton's exposition of the Antislavery Project was published in *Sixth Annual Report of the Executive Committee of the American Antislavery Society . . .* (New York, 1839).

13. *Report on the Powers and Duties of Congress upon the Subjects of Slavery and the Slave Trade* (Boston, 1838).

14. William Jay, *View of the Actions of the Federal Government with Regard to Slavery* (1839).

15. Antislavery radicals like Joshua Giddings called for the abolition of the coastal slave trade, as did the Liberty Party in 1844. In the 1850s Lincoln called for federal suppression of slavery on the high seas, but he never said whether that included suppression of the coastwise slave trade. His imposition of a naval blockade at the outset of the Civil War rendered the issue moot, as it was designed to suppress all southern maritime commerce.

16. Schlesinger and Israel, eds., *American Presidential Elections*, 1: 801–7.

17. Schlesinger, ed., *American Presidential Elections*, 2: 902–5.

18. *Congressional Globe*, March 9, 1836, p. 289.

19. There are many studies of the gag rule debates, but some of the most comprehensive are in William W. Freehling, *The Road to Disunion: Secessionists at Bay, 1776–1854* (New York, 1990); William Lee Miller, *Arguing About Slavery: John Quincy Adams and the Great Battle in the United States Congress* (New York, 1995).

20. Quoted in Freehling, *The Road to Disunion: Secessionists at Bay*, p. 322.

21. *Remarks of Henry B. Stanton in the Representatives' Hall on the 23nd and 24th of February, Before the Committee of the House of Representatives of Massachusetts, To Whom was Referred Sundry Memorials on the Subject of Slavery* (Boston, 1837), pp. 6, 19–22, 26.

22. This was the basis of Weld's claim that slaves were entitled to due process. Under the Fifth Amendment a slave could not be deprived of property in his or her self without due process of law. Theodore Dwight Weld, *The Power of Congress over the District of Columbia* (New York, 1838), pp. 39, 40.

23. William Slade, *Speech of Mr. Slade, of Vermont, on the abolition of slavery and the slave trade in the District of Columbia: delivered in the House of Representatives of the U.S. December 20, 1837: to which is added the intended conclusion of the speech, suppressed by resolution of the House,* p. 21.

24. Richard Lawrence Miller, *Lincoln and His World, Volume 2: Prairie Politician, 1834–1842* (Mechanicsburg, PA, 2008), pp. 139-42.

25. For the assembly vote of January 20, 1837, see *Journal of the Tenth General Assembly of the State of Illinois,* p. 311.

26. *Journal of the Tenth General Assembly of the State of Illinois,* March 3, 1837, pp. 817–18. Emphasis added.

27. Quoted in Burlingame, *Abraham Lincoln: A Life,* 1: 122.

28. *Congressional Globe,* January 10, 1849, p. 212. When it became clear that the committee would not act on Lincoln's resolution, he announced his intention to introduce the bill himself but abandoned the idea when his backers abandoned him. See *CW,* 2: 20–21. Burlingame, *Abraham Lincoln: A Life,* 1: 286–93; Kenneth J. Winkle, *Lincoln's Citadel: The Civil War in Washington, D.C.* (New York, 2013), 49–57.

29. Rodney O. Davis and Douglas L. Wilson, eds., *The Lincoln-Douglas Debates* (Galesburg, IL, 2008), p. 48.

30. *Congressional Globe,* April 2, 1861, p. 1497. The best account of the abolition of slavery in Washington, DC, is Kate Masur, *An Example for All the Land: Emancipation and the Struggle over Equality in Washington, D.C.* (Chapel Hill, 2010).

31. Henry Wilson, *Rise and Fall of the Slave Power in America,* vol. 3 (Boston and New York, 1877), p. 276.

32. *CW,* 5: 192.

33. Schlesinger, ed, *American Presidential Elections,* 2: 1039–43.

34. *CW,* 2: 451.

35. David and Wilson, ed., *Lincoln-Douglas Debates,* p. 47.

36. Schlesinger, ed., *American Presidential Elections,* 2: 1126.

37. *CW*, 2: 300.

38. On the incoherence of the *Prigg* decision, see Pinsker, "After 1850." For *Prigg* as a proslavery decision, see Paul Finkelman, "*Prigg v. Pennsylvania* and Northern State Courts: Anti-Slavery Use of a Proslavery Decision," *Civil War History* 25, no. 1 (March 1979): 5–35; Finkelman, *Supreme Injustice: Slavery in the Nation's Highest Court* (Cambridge, MA, 2018), pp. 140–71. Among recent scholars who see a more complex decision, see Leslie Friedman Goldstein, "A 'Triumph of Freedom' After All? Prigg v. Pennsylvania Re-examined," *Law and History Review* 29 (2011); H. Robert Baker, "A Better Story in *Prigg v. Pennsylvania?*" *Journal of Supreme Court History* 39 (July 2014).

39. On the discretion localities exercised in policing the written law, see Laura F. Edwards, "The Legal World of Elizabeth Bagby's Commonplace Book: Federalism, Women, and Governance," *Journal of the Civil War Era* 9, no. 4 (December 2019): 504–23.

40. *Prigg* v. *Pennsylvania*, 41 US (16 Pet.) 539 (1842). The ambiguity of Story's decision has led scholars to read it in very different ways. Paul Finkelman has long argued that Story wrote an "infamous" proslavery decision. See, most recently, Finkelman, *Supreme Injustice: Slavery in the Nation's Highest Court* (Cambridge, MA, 2018), pp. 140–68. But see also Goldstein, "A 'Triumph of Freedom' After All?" pp. 763–96.

41. Quotations in this paragraph are from R. J. M. Blackett, *The Captive's Quest for Freedom: Fugitive Slaves, the 1850 Fugitive Slave Law, and the Politics of Slavery* (Cambridge, UK, 2018), pp. 14, 75. For a broader account of the changing political significance of fugitive slaves, see Edward B. Rugemer, *Slave Law and the Politics of Resistance in the Early Atlantic World* (Cambridge, MA, 2018).

42. *U.S. Statutes at Large*, 31st Cong., 1st Sess., pp. 462–65.

43. *Congressional Globe*, January 4, 1850 (appendix), p. 79; February 13–14, 1850 (appendix), p. 150.

44. Blackett, *Captive's Quest*, pp. 20, 32, 15.

45. Blackett, *Captive's Quest*, p. 10.

46. The Union army adopted the same tactic in the first year of the Civil War. When slaveholders or their representatives arrived at military camps demanding the return of their slaves, Union offi-

cers often demanded substantial documentation as a means of thwarting the rendition.

47. Blackett, *Captive's Quest*, pp. 36–37.
48. *CW*, 2, p. 233*n*.
49. *CW*, 4: 152, 153, 154.
50. *CW*, 4: 152–54.
51. William H. Seward to Abraham Lincoln, December 26, 1860, *ALP-LC*. A transcription of the letter appears in Frederick W. Seward, *Seward at Washington: Senator and Secretary of State. A Memoir of his Life with Selections From his Letters. 1846–1861* (New York, 1891) pp. 484–85.
52. *CW*, 4: 264.
53. *CW*, 4: 269.
54. *CW*, 2: 321.
55. *CW*, 2: 515.
56. *CW*, 2: 408. Lincoln's views on Black citizenship are treated more fully in chapter 3.
57. *CW*, 2: 501.
58. *CW*, 2: 452.
59. For Lincoln's view of the founders' intentions, see *CW*, 2: 492.
60. *CW*, 2: 471.
61. *CW*, 2: 551.
62. *CW*, 2: 230.
63. *CW*, 8: 41.
64. For recent scholarship more or less endorsing this view, see James L. Huston, *The British Gentry, the Southern Planter, and the Northern Family Farmer: Agriculture and Sectional Antagonism in North America* (Baton Rouge, 2015). Huston argues, plausibly in my view, that whereas high wages for northern agricultural laborers made it possible for them to save and buy farms of their own, hundreds of thousands of southern yeoman were forced out of the slave states because of the virtual land monopoly of the southern planters and the stifling effect of the plantations on economic opportunity in the South.
65. *CW*, 2: 352, 365.
66. *CW*, 1: 347–48. Emphasis added.
67. *CW*, 2: 263–64. Emphasis added.
68. As the foremost student of Lincoln's economic views explains, Lin-

coln's belief that "contained slavery would die" was "a self-evident truth to him, implicit in his entire economic thought, and had little to do with soil depletion or other less fundamental factors of which he was also aware. American prosperity, the greatest in the history of man, was the fruit of social mobility, of the clear path to all. The absence of this principle caused economic decline. Deprived of the artificial and by definition temporary stimulus of expansion, the slave economy had to decline." The unprofitability of slavery would in turn lead planters to "turn out of self-interest to the free labor system." Gabor S. Boritt, *Lincoln and the Economics of the American Dream* (Urbana, IL, 1978) p. 163.

69. *CW*, 2: 318, 204.
70. *CW*, 2: 318.
71. *CW*, 2: 462.
72. *CW*, 2: 488, 446, 263.
73. *CW*, 2: 318.
74. *CW*, 2: 318.
75. William F. Moore and Jane Ann Moore, *Collaborators for Emancipation: Abraham Lincoln and Owen Lovejoy* (Champaign, IL, 2013).
76. *CW*, 2: 468.
77. *CW*, 2: 458–59.
78. *CW*, 3: 144–45.
79. *CW*, 3: 351.
80. *CW*, 3: 384–86. Lincoln's overriding concern with attracting "discordant" elements into the Republican Party is a familiar theme among historians. A thorough recent account is Sidney Blumenthal, *The Political Life of Abraham Lincoln, Volume 3: All the Powers of the Earth, 1856–1860* (New York, 2019), esp. part 2.
81. Schlesinger, ed., *American Presidential Elections*, 2: 1039–41.
82. Schlesinger, ed., *American Presidential Elections*, 2: 1124–27.

4. "My Ancient Faith"

1. Don E. Fehrenbacher, *The Dred Scott Case: Its Significance in American Law and Politics* (New York, 1978).
2. For the text of Taney's decision, see https://www.law.cornell.edu/supremecourt/text/60/393#writing-USSC_CR_0060_0393_ZO.

3. https://www.law.cornell.edu/supremecourt/text/60/393#writing -USSC_CR_0060_0393_ZO.

4. https://www.law.cornell.edu/supremecourt/text/60/393#writing -USSC_CR_0060_0393_ZD1.

5. https://www.law.cornell.edu/supremecourt/text/60/393#writing -USSC_CR_0060_0393_ZD1.

6. https://www.law.cornell.edu/supremecourt/text/60/393#writing -USSC_CR_0060_0393_ZD.

7. Kenneth M. Stampp, *America in 1858: A Nation on the Brink* (New York, 1990), p. 104.

8. For a similar interpretation by a recent scholar, see Mark A. Graber, *Dred Scott and the Problem of Constitutional Evil* (Cambridge, UK, 2006).

9. Aptheker, *A Documentary History of the Negro People in the United States*, p. 392.

10. Suffrage Convention of the Colored Citizens of New York, Troy, September 14, 1858. See http://coloredconventions.org/items/show/239

11. *CW*, 2: 403–4.

12. *CW*, 2: 264.

13. *CW*, 3: 445–46.

14. *CW*, 2: 222–23.

15. *CW*, 3: 399.

16. *CW*, 2: 500–501.

17. Stephen Douglas, for example, operated within the same classical economic premises but was defiantly indifferent to the evil of slavery. When he claimed that slavery would never expand into the desert southwest he was effectively saying that the fate of slavery should be determined by the market for slaves.

18. Robert Steinfeld, *The Invention of Free Labor: The Employment Relation in English and American Law and Culture, 1350–1870* (Chapel Hill, 1991). Critics of the classical liberal conception of freedom point out that a contract, however voluntarily entered, could create highly unequal and exploitative relationships. On the particular inequality of the marriage contract, see Amy Dru Stanley, *From Bondage to Contract: Wage Labor, Marriage, and the Market in the Age of Emancipation* (Cambridge UK, 1998). More generally,

see the powerful critique by Christopher Tomlins, *Freedom Bound: Law, Labor, and Civic Identity in Colonizing English America, 1580– 1865* (New York, 2010). Fortunately, contractual freedom did not exist in isolation from more robust definitions. A commitment to equality, for example, has often thickened the thinness of a strictly contractual freedom. On the contested notions of freedom, see Eric Foner, *The Story of American Freedom* (New York, 1998).

19. *CW*, 2: 405.
20. *CW*, 2: 233*n*.
21. *CW*, 2: 403.
22. *CW*, 2: 453.
23. *CW*, 2: 462, 464.
24. *CW*, 3: 9.
25. *CW*, 3: 112.
26. *CW*, 3: 177–78. See also *CW*, 3: 268, 274.
27. *CW*, 4: 179, 299–300.
28. *CW*, 4: 263–64.
29. All quotations of Bates in this and subsequent paragraphs are taken from *Opinion of Attorney General Bates on Citizenship* (Washington, DC, 1863).
30. *CW*, 2: 452.
31. *CW*, 2: 452.
32. *CW*, 3: 78, 80.
33. *CW*, 3: 116.
34. *CW*, 3: 145–46.
35. *CW*, 3: 19.
36. *CW*, 3: 380.
37. *CW*, 2: 256.
38. *CW*, 5: 372.
39. The best account of colonization is Eric Foner, "Lincoln and Colonization," in Eric Foner, ed, *Our Lincoln: New Perspectives on Lincoln and His World* (New York, 2008), pp. 135–66. Foner sees colonization, correctly in my view, as one piece of Lincoln's larger emancipation policy. This point is elaborated in Chapter 5.
40. [39] On the racial pessimism of the colonizationists, see Polgar, *Standard Bearers of Equality*.

5. The Forfeiture of Rights

1. William Whiting, *The War Powers of the President and the Legislative Powers of Congress in Relation to Rebellion, Treason, and Slavery*, 2d ed. (Boston, 1862), p. 51.
2. E. P. Thompson, *The Making of the English Working Class* (London, 1964), p. 24.
3. *CW*, 3: 454.
4. Andrew Kent, "The Constitution and the Laws of War During the Civil War" *Notre Dame Law Review*, Vol. 85, no. 5 (2010), pp. 1853ff.
5. James G. Randall, *Constitutional Problems Under Lincoln*, rev. ed. (Champaign, IL, 1951). Randall was a leading proponent of Civil War "revisionism," the school of thought that, among other things, systematically erased all evidence of the antislavery origins of the war. Consequently, his pioneering study contains no reference at all to antislavery constitutionalism. More recent legal or constitutional histories of the Civil War era perpetuate the erasure. For two examples, see the otherwise exemplary G. Edward White, *Law in American History: From the Colonial Years Through the Civil War* (New York, 2012). Laura Edwards, *A Legal History of the Civil War and Reconstruction* (New York, 2015), in which antislavery constitutionalism scarcely exists. A partial exception is Timothy S. Huebner, *Liberty and Union: The Civil War Era in American Constitutionalism* (Lawrence, KS, 2016). Huebner grasps the broad outlines of antislavery constitutionalism but misses its prewar origins. I have made preliminary attempts to reconstruct the history and significance of antislavery constitutionalism in *Freedom National* and *The Scorpion's Sting*.
6. *Congressional Globe*, April 15, 1842, p. 429.
7. Francis P. Blair Sr., *Republican Documents: Letter from Francis P. Blair. to My Neighbors* (New York: Printed by the *New York Evening Post*, nd), 7. Quoted in Andrew F. Hammann, "Emancipation and Exclusion: The Politics of Slavery and Colonization, 1787–1865 (PhD dissertation; Stanford University, 2017), p. 274.
8. Joshua Giddings, *The Exiles of Florida, or, the Crimes Committed by Our Government against the Maroons . . .* (Columbus, OH, 1858), p. 143.
9. George E. Baker, ed., *The Works of William H. Seward* (New York, 1853), 1: 195.

10. Baker, ed., *Works of William H. Seward*, 1: 86.

11. Baker, ed., *Works of William H. Seward*, vol. 4 (Boston, 1884), p. 237.

12. Baker, ed., *Works of William H. Seward*, 4: 660.

13. William Jay, *A View of the Action of the Federal Government, in Behalf of Slavery*, 2nd ed. (New York, 1839), 222–23.

14. *Congressional Globe*, 36: 2 (appendix), pp. 66, 83, 129. Southern congressmen denounced these references to the Adams doctrine and demanded that Republicans repudiate them, which Republicans refused to do. See, for example, the exchange between Simms and Curtis in *Congressional Globe*, February 26, 1861, p. 1231.

15. Orville H. Browning to Abraham Lincoln, April 30, 1861, *ALP-LC*.

16. *Statutes at Large*, 32nd Cong., 1st Sess., July 13, 1861, p. 257.

17. The agency of the slaves in their own emancipation is now widely, though not universally, accepted among historians. As far back as the 1930s pioneering scholars were stressing the importance of wartime slave resistance. See especially W. E. Burghardt Du Bois, *Black Reconstruction in America* (New York, 1935), and Bell Irvin Wiley, *Southern Negroes, 1861–1865* (New Haven, 1938). Slave resistance was revived as a general theme in the shadow of World War II. See especially Herbert Aptheker, *American Negro Slave Revolts* (New York, 1943), and Kenneth M. Stampp, *The Peculiar Institution: Slavery in the Antebellum South* (New York, 1956). This theme became pervasive in slavery studies beginning in the 1970s. By then a number of historians had begun to relate slave resistance to wartime emancipation. See especially John Hope Franklin, *The Emancipation Proclamation* (Garden City, NY, 1963), and Leon F. Litwack, *Been in the Storm So Long: The Aftermath of Slavery* (New York, 1979). Armstead L. Robinson, *Bitter Fruits of Bondage: The Demise of Slavery and the Collapse of the Confederacy, 1861–1865* (Charlottesville, 2004), is particularly good on the political significance of slave resistance during the Civil War. Among the more recent studies emphasizing slave agency in the emancipation process, see Steven Hahn, *The Political Worlds of Slavery and Freedom* (Cambridge, MA, 2009); Stephanie McCurry, *Confederate Reckoning: Power and Politics in the Civil War South* (Cambridge, MA, 2010); and Oakes, *Freedom National*. For a critique of the scholarship on popular resistance within the Confederacy, see Gary Gallagher, *The Confederate War*

(Cambridge, MA, 1999), which focuses on non-slaveholder support for the southern war effort rather than slave resistance.

The agency of the slaves was definitively established by the Freedmen and Southern Society Project (FSSP) at the University of Maryland. Ira Berlin, et al., eds., *Freedom: The Destruction of Slavery: A Documentary History of Emancipation, 1861–1872* (New York, 1986). Dozens of books and essays have been inspired by this work. Indeed, all those who study emancipation, myself included, operate within the shadow of this extraordinary project, whose documents capture the myriad ways in which emancipation played out on the ground in the Civil War South. But because the documents begin in 1861 they cannot capture the origins of emancipation in the prewar antislavery movement, especially the close relationship between the fugitive slave crisis of the 1850s and wartime emancipation. And because the FSSP documents are organized geographically rather than chronologically, they have the added effect of obscuring the sequence of emancipation policy moves as they developed in Washington, DC. This can sometimes lead to an incomplete appreciation of the policies that the documents reveal, albeit inadvertently and often obliquely. No doubt a singular focus on the evolution of policy can efface the complexity and variety of ways emancipation was experienced on the ground, just as a singular emphasis on the endless variety of individual experiences of emancipation can obscure the origins and evolution of an increasingly radical antislavery policy. Ideally, a full appreciation of emancipation takes both aspects of the process into account. Otherwise it is hard to capture the political significance of slave resistance. For two recent studies, both thoroughly researched, emphasizing myriad experiences over radicalizing policy, see Amy Murrell Taylor, *Embattled Freedom: Journeys through the Civil War's Refugee Camps* (Chapel Hill, 2018), and Joseph P. Reidy, *Illusions of Emancipation: The Pursuit of Freedom and Equality in the Twilight of Slavery* (Chapel Hill, 2019).

18. Butler to Lieutenant General Winfield Scott, May 25, 1861, in Benjamin F. Butler, *Private and Official Correspondence of Gen. Benjamin F. Butler, During the Period of the Civil War,* vol. 1 (Norwood, MA, 1917), p. 107. Hereafter cited as *Butler Correspondence.*

19. *OR*, ser. 2, vol. 1, pp. 754–55.
20. Butler to Simon Cameron, June 29, 1861, *Butler Correspondence*, 1: 188.
21. Quoted in Winkle, *Lincoln's Citadel*, p. 238.
22. Ira Berlin, et al., eds., *Freedom: A Documentary History of Emancipation*, series 1, volume 1: *The Destruction of Slavery* (Cambridge, 1985), p. 78.
23. For the abolitionist response to one part of Cushing's opinion, see Gautham Rao, "The Federal 'Posse Comitatus' Doctrine: Slavery, Compulsion, and Statecraft in Mid-Nineteenth-Century America," *Law and History Review* 26, No. 1 (Spring 2008): 26–31.
24. Opinion of Senator Bishop. *Jack, a Negro Man,* v. *Mary Martin.* 14 Wend, 507; 1835 N.Y. LEXIS 3.
25. James C. Alvord, "Trial by Jury, in Questions of Personal Freedom," *American Jurist and Law Magazine* 17 (1837): 94–113.
26. *OR*, ser. 2, p. 757.
27. *OR*, ser. 2, pp. 756–57.
28. Charles B. Calvert to Abraham Lincoln, July 10, 1861, *ALP-LC*.
29. Theodore Calvin Pease and James G. Randall, eds., *The Diary of Orville Hickman Browning, Volume I: 1850–1864* (Springfield, IL, 1925), p. 478.
30. *OR*, ser. 2, vol. 1, p. 760. The document quoted here was written by General Scott's secretary, Schuyler Hamilton. It is not entirely clear whether the words Hamilton put in quotation marks were Scott's or Lincoln's. But there is no reason to doubt that they accurately convey Lincoln's wishes.
31. *OR*, ser. 2, vol. 1, p. 760. General Orders 33 went out the next day, July 17. "*Fugitive slaves* will under no pretext whatever be permitted to reside or be in any way harbored in the quarters and camps of the troops serving in this department." Emphasis added.
32. *The Statutes at Large, Treaties, and Proclamations of the United States of America*, vol. XII (Boston, 1863), p. 319. The sidebar to the crucial Section 4 of the law reads: "When claims to persons held to service and labor to be forfeited."
33. *OR*, ser. 2, vol. 1, pp. 761–62.
34. Even before the Blue Jug was built opponents of slavery complained about the use of Washington jails to house slaves. Charles Miner,

1829, House resolution advocating abolition in Washington, DC, complained, "That the public prisons have been extensively used (perverted from the purposes for which they were erected) for carrying on the domestic slave-trade." *Register of Debates*, January 6, 1829, p. 167.

35. Quoted in Masur, *Equal Before the Law*, quotation on manuscript page 313. My account of the controversy over the Blue Jug relies heavily on Masur.

36. Report of the Committee on the District of Columbia, June 21, 1862 37th Cong., 2nd Sess, in *Reports of Committees: 30th Congress, 1st Session – 48th Congress, 2nd Session* (Washington, DC).

37. *Congressional Globe*, December 4, 1861, p. 10.

38. *OR*, ser. 2, vol. 1, p. 783. Emphasis added.

39. *Congressional Globe*, January 28, 1850, p. 236.

40. *Washington Evening Star*, January 30, 1862.

41. *OR*, ser. 1, vol. 1, p. 467.

42. *CW*, 4: 506, 517–18.

43. *CW*, 4: 531.

44. Fred Albert Shannon, *The Organization and Administration of the Union Army, 1861–1865*, vol. 1 (Gloucester, MA, 1928; 1965), pp. 58ff.

45. It is often suggested that Lincoln fired Frémont because of the emancipation order, but the only evidence for this is chronology. Frémont issued the order in early September and was removed in late October. This chronological fallacy is easily exposed. By late October Union troops were legally emancipating slaves in western Missouri with Lincoln's blessing.

46. Some months later, transferred to South Carolina, Hunter would issue an order similar to Frémont's, which Lincoln would similarly revoke, though Hunter retained his command. Edward A. Miller Jr., *Lincoln's Abolitionist General: The Biography of David Hunter* (Columbia, SC, 1997).

47. *Hannibal Daily Messenger*, November 28, 1861.

48. On Lane's activities in Kansas, see Nicole Etcheson, *Bleeding Kansas: Contested Liberty in the Civil War Era* (Lawrence, KS, 2004).

49. The Kentucky senator was clearly trying to neutralize Congressman Owen Lovejoy's antislavery resolution, passed a week earlier by Republicans in the House, which had declared that it was not

the business of anyone in the Union army or navy to participate in any way in the capture and return of fugitive slaves. Where Lovejoy's resolution, which passed overwhelmingly, cleared the path to military emancipation by making Union camps and ships attractive havens for fugitive slaves, Powell's failed alternative would have made military emancipation impossible.

50. *Congressional Globe,* July 18, 1861, pp. 186–87. Asked to reduce his amendment to writing, Lane reworded it to read: "Unless it be necessary in enforcing the laws, or maintaining the Constitution of the Union."

51. Letter dated October 3, 1861, from Mounds, Missouri, published in the Columbus, Ohio, *Crisis,* October 31, 1861.

52. *Daily Missouri Democrat,* October 21, 1861.

53. *New York Times* report, quoted in the *New Hampshire Patriot and State Gazette,* November 27, 1861.

54. *Salem Observer,* October 26, 1861.

55. New Orleans *True Delta,* October 27, 1861. Emphasis added.

56. *Leavenworth Daily Conservative,* December 11, 1861.

57. *CW,* 5:48. Emphasis added.

58. Edward McPherson, *The Political History of the United States During the Great Rebellion,* 2nd ed. (Washington, DC, 1965) pp. 249, 416. Emphasis added.

59. Springfield (MA) *Republican,* December 5, 1861. Lincoln's reluctance to enlist Black soldiers, which persisted into the summer of 1862, should not be confused with reluctance to emancipate—for which there is no evidence.

60. *Senate Executive Documents,* No. 2, 37th Cong, 2nd Sess., p. 13.

61. Quoted in Oakes, *Freedom National,* p. 207.

62. *Annual Report of the Secretary of the Navy,* December 1861 (Washington, DC, 1861), pp. 20–21.

63. On the variety of emancipation experiences, see Reidy, *Illusions of Emancipation.* On the division over emancipation between Democrats and Republicans in the Union army, see Jonathan W. White, *Emancipation, the Union Army, and the Reelection of Abraham Lincoln* (Baton Rouge, 2014).

64. *Congressional Globe,* December 18, 1861, pp. 130–31.

65. *Congressional Globe,* December 18, 1861, pp. 130–31.

66. *OR*, ser. 2, vol. 1, p. 235.
67. On December 11 New York congressman Lansing introduced a resolution denouncing Halleck's order "prohibiting negroes from coming within the lines of the army" and pointed out that "a different policy and practice prevails in other departments, by the direct sanction of the Administration." McPherson, *Political History of the United States*, 254.
68. *New York Tribune*, January 21, 1861.
69. *New York Tribune*, January 23, 1862.
70. *New York World*, January 29, 1862. Emphasis added.
71. *New York Tribune*, February 12, 1862.

6. "A King's Cure"

1. *Sixth Annual Report of the Executive Committee of the American Anti-Slavery Society* (New York, 1839), pp. 11–19.
2. Leonard L. Richards, *The Slave Power: The Free North and Southern Domination, 1780–1860* (Baton Rouge, 2000); Corey M. Brooks, *Liberty Power: Antislavery Third Parties and the Transformation of American Politics* (Chicago, 2016).
3. *Congressional Globe*, February 13 and 14, 1850 (appendix), pp. 149–50.
4. William W. Freehling and Craig M. Simpson, eds., *Secession Debated: Georgia's Showdown in 1860* (New York, 1992).
5. Stanley Harrold, *The Abolitionists and the South, 1831–1861* (Lexington, KY, 1995).
6. *CW*, 5: 29–31.
7. *CW*, 5: 145.
8. *CW*, 5: 145.
9. *CW*, 5: 318.
10. Louis P. Masur, *Lincoln's Hundred Days: The Emancipation Proclamation and the War for the Union* (Cambridge, MA, 2012), pp. 187–899.
11. *CW*, 6: 291.
12. *CW*, 6: 358–59.
13. *CW*, 6: 440.
14. *CW*, 6: 364–66.
15. *CW*, 7: 1–2. Notwithstanding the tremendous war powers Lincoln

claimed as commander in chief, he still did not believe he had the authority to order a disloyal state like Louisiana to abolish slavery as a condition for readmission to the Union. Even in late 1865 President Andrew Johnson would not formally *require* South Carolina or any of the defeated states to ratify the Thirteenth Amendment. Instead, Johnson's secretary of state, William Seward, let it be known that ratification was what Johnson expected from those states returning to the Union.

16. Scott Ackerman, "'We Are Abolitionizing the West': The Union Army and the Implementation of Federal Emancipation Policy, 1861–1865" (PhD dissertation, Graduate Center of the City University of New York, 2019).

17. *CW*, 7: 51.

18. *CW*, 7: 126.

19. *CW*, 7: 141–42, 154–55, 161.

20. Francis Newton Thorpe, *The Federal and State Constitutions, Colonial Charters, and Other Organic Laws of the States, Territories, and Colonies . . .* , vol. 1 (Washington, DC, 1909), pp. 295–96.

21. *CW*, 7: 226.

22. *New York Times*, March 11, 1864.

23. Charles L. Wagant, *The Mighty Revolution: Negro Emancipation in Maryland, 1862–1864* (Baltimore, 1964), p. 223.

24. *CW*, 8: 148.

25. The previous spring Lincoln himself had been noticeably slow to support the amendment, but after his reelection he threw himself wholeheartedly into the effort to get it passed by the House.

26. Few historians any longer dispute the significance of slave resistance during the Civil War, but most of the focus has been on the importance of slave subversion and Black troops for federal antislavery policy. There are also excellent state studies. But there is as yet no study demonstrating the indirect but crucial impact slave resistance had on making a Thirteenth Amendment feasible, thanks to the number of states that abolished slavery.

27. *A Documentary History of the Constitution of the United States of America*, vol. 2 (Washington, DC, 1894), pp. 530–601.

28. *CW*, 8: 254–55.

Index

256 Index

Weld, Theodore Dwight, 35, 68, 221n
Welles, Gideon, 168–69
Western Department, 161
West Virginia, xxix, 185, 201, 202
Whig Party, 26, 34–35, 57, 65–66, 65–66 26, 83, 94, 96
whippings, xiii
white supremacy, xiii, xxv–xxvi, 122–25, 178
Whiting, William, 134
Wilmot, David, 42, 73–74

Wilmot Proviso, xxi, 42–43, 73–74
Wilson, Henry, 155–56
Wilson, James, 17
Wirt, William, 117
Wisconsin Territory, 99–100, 101
Wise, Henry, 66
women's rights, xiv, 111, 122
work ethic, 110–11
Wright, Henry C., 81

Yates, William, 47
yeoman farmers, 223n